Table of Contents

EXAMINATION CONTENT OUTLINE
FOR NORTH CAROLINA REAL ESTATE LICENSING EXAMINATION

The exam consists of 140 graded questions; 100 scored National questions and 40 scored State question You may also be given up to 5 additional questions that are being evaluated for possible future exam use You will not know if you are answering a scored test question or a question that is being evaluated for possible future use (which will not count towards your final grade). **In order to receive a passing sco you must answer 71 out of the 100 National questions correctly and 29 out of the 40 graded State questions correctly.** The National and State questions will be combined into one examination. You ma use a hand-held battery operated calculator that does not have alphabetic capabilities on the exam.

You will have 4 hours to complete the entire examination. You must pass both sections in order to obta your Provisional License. If you pass one section but not the other you will only need to retest and pass the section that you missed. In this case, you will have 2.5 hours to take the National portion of the test or 1.5 hours to take the State portion of the test.

It is highly recommended that you obtain a copy of the **Real Estate Licensing in North Carolina** publication, available on the Commission website (www.ncrec.gov) – https://www.ncrec.gov/Licensing/ApplyLicense.

IMPORTANT TIPS AND SUGGESTIONS

The examination is a standardized test and therefore you should never leave a question blank. Make su to read all answer choices carefully and note "yes", "no" or "maybe" on your scratch paper. Remember i you can eliminate 2 wrong answers, you have a 50/50 chance of selecting the correct answer. You can skip a question and return to it later if you are not sure how to answer. If you are unsure of how to answer a math problem, if possible, try to work the problem backwards by using the answers provided. recommend that you start with answer choice "C" and then you can determine if the answer needs to be higher or lower.

In preparation for the examination you need to study and **memorize** all KEY facts outlined in this

workbook. Important topics will have a ⚠ symbol which will indicate heavily tested items that mus be learned. The workbook has multiple questions to help focus your review. Make sure you read the solutions at the end of the key points review.

EAL PROPERTY OWNERSHIP AND INTEREST

al Property, Personal Property and Fixtures

- <u>Real Property</u> includes the "Bundle of Rights" + real estate. It is immovable and includes the land and everything attached to the land. Homes, buildings, lots and trees are all examples of real property. Transferred by deed.
- <u>Personal Property</u> includes all movable property that is not considered real property. When purchasing real property where a buyer seeks personal property (refrigerator, washer/dryer) it must be included in the Offer to Purchase and Contract. Personal property can be sold through a <u>bill of sale</u>, and is sometimes referred to as personalty or chattel. Furniture, clothes, vehicles are all examples of personal property.

     A manufactured (mobile) home can be personal – registered with the DMV or real property – attached to a permanent foundation, with hitch and wheels removed, on land that is owned and DMV title is cancelled.

- <u>Fixture</u> – An item that was once personal property however is now considered to be real property based upon a set of circumstances. Common examples include HVAC equipment, light fixtures, fences and landscaping (not in moveable containers). To determine if an item is real or personal you must apply the **Total Circumstances Test.**

    Remember – I.R.M.A – <u>Listed in order of priority</u>:

    Final expression of agreement

  - Intention of the party
  - Relationship of the attacher (owner vs. renter)
  - Method (will it cause damage when removed)
  - Adaptation (custom built for that location – such as a built-in appliance)
  - NOTE: It is important to remember that Agreement trumps all of the above. A buyer and seller that are negotiating a contract can agree that personal property is to stay or a fixture may be severed. Failure to include a provision in the Offer to Purchase and Contract for personal property such as a refrigerator, will result in a loss to the buyer as the seller will not be obligated to leave it. Failure to exclude a fixture, such as an antique chandelier, will result in a loss to the seller, as they will be obligated to leave the fixture with the property.

     The weight, size, value or location of the item is irrelevant when determining if an item is a fixture. The Real Estate Commission receives a significant number of complaints on this topic. If a seller wants to keep an item that is a fixture (antique chandelier, hot tub) it must be specifically excluded in the Purchase and Sale Contract.

  Additional Important Topics:

- <u>Trade Fixtures</u> – will remain personal property of the tenant as long as they are removed by the end of the lease. These items are used in a trade or business such as a restaurant with brick ovens and exhaust fans.
- <u>Agricultural Fixtures</u> – must remain with the property at the end of lease unless they have been specifically excluded.

- o Uniform Commercial Code – is a security interest in a fixture such that it remains personal property until payment has been made in full. In the event of default the creditor can repossess the property.

     Appurtenance – For national exam purposes an appurtenance is an improvement on the land. It is a right or privilege that runs with the land (transfers to the new owner).

Real Property Rights of Ownership

- o <u>Riparian Rights</u> – Running Water – River or Stream, Lake (no tide) or Pond – land that borders a body of water.
    - ➢ Navigable – Own to the banks and the State controls access. Permission to build a dock would need to be obtained from the State; So, an owner "*may*" be able to build a dock or **"may not"**.
    - ➢ Non-Navigable – Own to the center of the body of water.
- o <u>Littoral Rights</u> – Large Lakes and Oceans – land that borders a body of water that has a tide. Owner's property line extends to the mean (average) high water mark and the State controls the foreshore. The public has the right to access the foreshore and water as long as they do not cross through private property.

     For national exam purposes – the doctrine of prior appropriation may be tested. The first party to use the water has the first right to the water. This doctrine is generally used in the western half of the country while riparian rights are used in the eastern half of the country.

     The rights afforded to a property that borders a navigable body of water remain with the property. The previous owner cannot retain rights to access water following closing – a the state controls the waterway and the property line extends to the banks of the river.

- o The boundaries along waterways can shift based on naturally occurring events.
- o <u>Accretion</u> – is the gradual adding of land through the accumulation of soil (the soil may be referr to as Alluvium/Alluvion). <u>Reliction</u> – is the gradual increase in land when water recedes (dries up). <u>Erosion</u> – is the gradual loss of land (think Grand Canyon). <u>Avulsion</u> – is the sudden / viole loss of land (perhaps from a hurricane or flood).

     The property line does not change under avulsion. The owner often is allowed to resto the land to its previous state within a limited period of time.

- o <u>Air Rights</u> – The right to the air above the property although it may be restricted by zoning rules An owner cannot demand that airplanes no longer fly over his/her land.
- o <u>Subsurface Rights</u> – The right to minerals, gas, or oil that are below the surface. These rights ma be separated or severed from the use of the land. An increased emphasis on these rights will be needed as fracking begins in NC. For example, an owner may have severed the mineral rights to property 50 years ago. The current owner of those rights may be able to frack the property without needing any approval from the current land owner. Property owners in North Carolina must complete the mandatory Mineral, Oil and Gas Disclosure form - disclosing severance of righ in the past or by the current owner.

Rights that have been severed typically would not automatically revert back to the current owner of the property upon death, bankruptcy or other catastrophic event.

 Subjacent / Lateral Support – any changes to a property cannot cause the loss of support for a neighbor. An owner cannot excavate their property without supporting the neighbors land.

Questions:

o When a seller fails to exclude a fixture from the Offer to Purchase and Contract such as a family heirloom, are they required to transfer it or can they replace the item with a similar quality fixture?

o A tenant is renting commercial space for a restaurant where trade fixtures have been installed. Upon termination of the lease can the tenant remove the trade fixtures? What if the trade fixtures are abandoned?

o What is the term that defines the sudden loss of land that would not result in a change in the property line?

Freehold and Leasehold Estates

o <u>Estate</u> – defined as the nature, degree, and extent of one's interest in real property that is possessory now or will be sometime in the future.

o <u>Freehold Estate</u> – an estate of indeterminable length that exists for a lifetime or longer. **These estates may be separated into inheritable vs non-inheritable estates. Inheritable:**

  ➤ **Fee Simple Absolute** – has ownership without a time limit and the rights to keep, sell, lease or encumber the property as he or she chooses. This is the **Highest and Best** form of ownership in real property.

  ➤ **Fee Simple Defeasible (or Qualified Fee)** – 1. Fee Simple Determinable – will **automatically** terminate upon the occurrence of some predetermined event **and** ownership will revert back to the original owner or heirs without the need of a lawsuit. 2. Fee Simple Conditional (or subject to a Condition Subsequent) – will **not automatically** terminate upon the occurrence of some predetermined event. Legal action must be taken in order for the original owner or his/her heirs to obtain legal title to the property (often through a **Suit to Quiet Title** – in order to establish superior title to the property).

  ➤ **Pur Autre Vie (For the Life of Another)** – a person is granted the rights to a property for as long as another person lives ("measuring life"). The property may be inherited until the measuring life dies and then the property is transferred to the remainderman.

  Non-Inheritable:

  o **Conventional Life Estate** – estate ends upon the death of the person to whom it was granted (life tenant) and reverts back to the owner or his/her heirs.

  o **Rights and Duties of a Life Tenant** – The life tenant may sell his/her interest, mortgage the property or rent the property but only for his/her lifetime. They are entitled to use timber for fuel and repairs (**estovers**), however they cannot profit by selling the timber or other resources. They must pay property taxes, make ordinary repairs and maintain insurance on the property.

- o **Homestead Exemption** – Limited to real estate that is occupied as the family home. Protects property from certain general liens such as judgments and debts (such as personal loans) but not from ad valorem property taxes, mortgage obligations or any other debt that is secured by the property. North Carolina provides for a limited exemption of $35,000 ($60,000 for certain unmarried individuals age 65 or older). The amount of the exemption varies by state and could require additional forms to be filed to qualify. A creditor may still be able to obtain a judgment against the property, however, if it is less than the limits noted above, they cannot force the sale of the property.

Non-Freehold Estates

<u>Leasehold Estate</u> – The right of temporary possession of a property, but not ownership. Lease contracts transfer with the property upon sale, unless otherwise the lease agreement states otherwise.

- o <u>Estate for Years</u> – provides for a definite end date. Does not have to be for a year but automatically terminates without notice.
- o <u>Estate from Year to Year</u> – a periodic tenancy that is indefinite in duration and automatically renews unless notice to terminate is given by either party. Typically month-to-month, however it can be for any period. Landlord or tenant may terminate by providing the agreed upon notice.
- o <u>Estate at Will</u> – may be terminated by either party at any time without notice. Indefinite length. (No married couples)
- o <u>Estate at Sufferance</u> – the tenant's right to possess the property terminated and they have failed to vacate. This typically occurs when the tenant stops paying rent. Eviction procedures are required to be followed and the landlord cannot "Self Help" by turning off utilities or changing the locks.
- o <u>Leasehold</u> – The tenants interest in the property. The tenant has a **hold** on the property as long as they pay rent.
- o <u>Leased Fee</u> – The owners interest in the property. The landlord is **paid the fee**. In addition to the leased fee interest, the owner retains a freehold estate, however possession of the property has been transferred to the tenant in return for $$.

Types of Ownership

A broker should be aware of how title can pass, however should never advise a client which title would be best in his/her situation. Only an attorney can advise a buyer as such a representation by a broker would result in the unauthorized practice of law.

- o <u>Severalty</u> – One person or entity. Business partnerships will take title in severalty.
- o <u>Concurrent Ownership</u> - More than one person or entity hold title.

➢ <u>Tenant-in-Common</u> – Two or more owners where ownership interest does not have to be equal. One tenant can encumber their interest in the property but not the whole. All owners have an equal right of possession and there is only 1 deed to the property. Upon death the owner's share transfers to his/her heirs through Probate. One owner can sell his/her interest to another party without approval, however would need all owners to agree to sell the entire property (unless Partition Action, also known as Suit for Partition - is sought through the courts). **This form of co-ownership would be used if you <u>DO NOT</u> want rights of survivorship (passing to other owners), rather having it pass to the heirs.**

➢ <u>Joint Tenancy</u> – Has unities – Same Time / Same Level of Ownership / from the Same Source. This type of ownership is not favored in North Carolina, however is used in other states so it is important to study the national rules. Joint tenants have the right of survivorship – meaning that if one dies his/her interest is passed to the remaining joint tenants not his/her heirs. A <u>will</u> cannot defeat joint tenancy. Only the sale of the joint tenant's interest will defeat the right of survivorship and the new tenant will own the interest as a Tenant-in-Common. **Joint tenancy is not shared with your kids (or heirs). You don't pass a JOINT to your kids.** North Carolina does not favor joint tenancy and therefore an attorney must include very specific language in a deed in order to obtain the right of survivorship. In NC it is possible to own the property in unequal amounts (as with tenants in common). It is recommended to know the <u>national</u> rules for testing purposes.

➢ <u>Tenancy by the Entirety</u> – Can only exist between a married couple. The surviving spouse automatically has the right of survivorship without passing through probate (courts). A will cannot defeat the right of survivorship. Divorce terminates Tenancy by the Entirety; The married couple will own as Tenants-in-Common. It is important to note that legal separation is not the same as divorce. Only divorce will terminate Tenancy by the Entirety.

 When a married couple purchases property in NC and fails to specify the type of ownership, they will own as Tenancy by the Entirety.

 It is very important to know what happens upon sale or death for each of the forms of ownership!! The sale of an owners share owned under joint tenancy will terminate his/her joint tenancy interest. The new owner will own as a tenant in common. The remaining joint tenants will not be affected.

brid Ownership

o <u>Condominium</u> – ownership of the airspace of the unit as well as co-ownership of the common areas. Created by recording a <u>declaration</u> and in North Carolina, upon the initial sale the buyer has <u>7 calendar days</u> to rescind the contract without penalty. Common elements can be for the use of all of the owners or there can be limited common elements (storage, garages, etc). Upon resale, the agent or the owner must provide the prospective purchaser with a <u>resale certificate</u> outlining the monthly common area expenses and fees. May be owned in severalty, tenants-in-common or tenancy by the entirety. In the event of a default by an owner that has a mortgage, the lender can foreclose on only the unit itself and not the condo complex. Owners are often required to pay HOA dues to cover common area expenses, which are a specific lien against the condo unit. Condos ca[n] be for residential, commercial (office) or industrial use.

- o Townhouse – ownership of the individual unit as well as the land that it rests upon including the party walls. The common areas are owned by the Homeowners Association.
- o Cooperative – Corporate owned property - The building is owned by a corporation and the purchaser receives a share of stock and a proprietary lease.
- o Timeshare – 5/5/5/10 – The purchaser has the right to use a property for at least 5 non-consecutive periods, over 5 or more years, has the right to terminate within 5 days of contract ar[d] developer must keep money in escrow account for 10 days. A timeshare developer can be fined $500 per occurrence for failure to follow the timeshare act (the only fine the NCREC can levy). A **project broker** supervises the licensees, similar to a broker-in-charge (see License Law and Commission Rules for additional requirements).

Questions:

- o Which forms of ownership contain the right of survivorship? What does the right of survivorshi[p] mean?
- o A married couple owns property under Tenancy by the Entirety, and have separated. What imp[act] will this have on the current form of ownership?
- o The owner of a condo defaults on his mortgage. What can the bank legally seek as a remedy?
- o Who owns the common elements in a townhome community?

Encumbrances to Real Property

Easements – a nonpossessory right or privilege in the land of another that should be in writing although it is not required. It does not create an ownership interest. Easements may be expressed (agreed to) or implied (born out of the action or conduct of the parties). Easements may be created by adverse possession, operation of law through condemnation, or by the action of the parties out o[f] *necessity* (the sale of a landlocked lot).

- o Appurtenant Easement – the right to use an adjacent lot (the properties must border each other) This easement runs with the land and is not disturbed by the sale or exchange by either party (unless the dominant or servient purchase the other lot). It creates a dominant estate – the own[er] that gets the benefit; and a servient estate – the owner that gets the burden. A common example would be a shared driveway that passes through one lot and into an adjoining lot. An easement [of] necessity becomes an appurtenant easement.
- o Easement in Gross – the right to use the property of another without the requirement that the lo[ts] adjoin. The easement may be personal or commercial.
  - ➢ Personal – Typically used for hunting or fishing. Cannot be assigned or inherited so when th[e] person dies the easement is automatically terminated.
  - ➢ Commercial – Typically granted to a business or entity with the right to assign or convey the interest. Examples include billboards, cell towers, railroad tracks or utilities. A commercial easement <u>will not</u> automatically terminate or revert to the current owner in the event of bankruptcy, sale or non-use.

- <u>Easement by Prescription</u> – (sometimes referred to as prescriptive easement or **adverse possession**) acquiring through hostile action by taking the property of another (7 years with color of title / 20 years without color of title. If continuous possession has occurred, they have a claim of right). Remember H.I. O.C.E.A.N. – Hostile. Intentional. Open. Continuous. Exclusive. Adverse. Notorious. Hostile means without the owner's permission. Non-use of a prescriptive easement will result in termination (as use must be continuous). The claimant will file a Suit to Quiet Title. Cannot claim property registered under the <u>Torrens system</u> – where title passes only when noted on the title certificate.

   You will need to memorize H.I. O.C.E.A.N. and apply it to fact situations. If a property owner gives permission to use the land then adverse possession cannot be claimed (no longer adverse). It is not necessary for the owner to know or be <u>aware</u> that someone has taken his/her land. It is presumed that an owner of property will monitor his/her land and take action against squatters before a claim can be made. There are no additional protections for an owner that is handicapped (blind, hermit, etc.).

   The party seeking the property can only claim the amount of the parcel they have actually taken. In a recent case (Minor v Minor, June 13, 2013)– one party tried to claim a 23 acre lot while only using 8 acres. The jury found against her claim of the entire lot as a claim arising out of adverse possession "is limited to the area actually possessed".

Questions:

- Is an owner protected from an adverse possession claim if they suffer from a handicap, making it difficult to detect?
- What is the difference between a lien and an encumbrance?
- Which form of co-ownership cannot be subject to a suit for partition?
- What law prevents a creditor from enforcing a lien against a property?
- _____ prevents a neighbor from causing damage to your property when excavating or mining his/her property?

License – permission to use a property that is not assignable or inheritable and can be revoked (typically used for hunting, fishing or the right to cross another's property). Automatically terminates upon death.

Encroachment – when an improvement crosses the property boundary line onto the property of another. Discovered with a survey.

Lis Pendens – a notice of pending litigation used to obtain an encumbrance against the property that is binding on future owners should the party win in a lawsuit against the current owner.

 Used to prevent an owner from transferring the property to someone else as the new owner would be liable should the current owner lose the court case.

Writ of Attachment – court ordered judgment that creates a general lien against real property. A writ of execution would be signed to force the sale of the property.

Governmental Rights in Land

- <u>Police Power</u> – The right to establish and enforce laws that set how land can be used (zoning, planning, building codes, environmental laws).
- <u>Eminent Domain</u> – The right to condemn private land for public use. Must be for the public good and requires fair compensation for the loss incurred (property's fair market value + damages). **Eminent domain is the RIGHT and condemnation is the PROCESS.**

 Lease agreements are terminated by condemnation.

- <u>Taxation</u> – The right to charge ad valorem property taxes (through the <u>Machinery Act</u> in NC) based upon a property's assessed value. In North Carolina, the assessed value is the market value, however municipalities are only required to revalue a property every 8 years. They can the assessed value every year. The machinery act establishes the right to charge taxes but <u>NOT the rate</u>. The city/county budget determines the rate. In addition to taxes municipalities can charge assessments for water and sewer lines, sidewalks, or streetlights. Taxes and assessments are superior to all other liens against a property including secured financing (mortgage, line of credit etc.).
- <u>Escheats</u> – The state cheats. Well not exactly, but that is how I remember it. The government's right to property when it has been abandoned (the owner dies without heirs).

 Property taxes attach to the property on January 1st, are due and payable on September 1st and are late after January 5th of the following year.

 Outside of North Carolina the "assessment rate system" may be used where the assessed value is equal to a percentage of the market value.

 Improvements made to the property such as building a new structure, building or an addition will be taxed in the next tax year. When construction for a new home begins after January 1 and completion occurs prior to the end of the year – the buyer will be taxed for just the land in the current year and will be taxed for the land and improvements in the following tax year. Additionally, the assessed value is not increased to the purchase price when the property is sold.

Land Use Restrictions

- <u>Restrictive / Protective Covenants</u> - a private land use restriction placed on a property (also called <u>Deed Restrictions</u>) usually placed by the developer to create <u>conformity</u> in a neighborhood. Restrictions are commonly for minimum square footage, architectural design, approved color schemes, etc. They are enforced by the homeowners' association (HOA) or by an owner within the neighborhood. Compliance is typically sought by the HOA by giving notice or seeking compliance through court action (<u>injunction</u> – to stop the offense). Restrictions run with the land upon transfer and are binding upon future owners.

- Can be terminated by 100% agreement of property owners in the subdivision (or some lesser amount outlined in the covenants).
- The right to enforce can be lost through <u>laches</u> where the HOA or homeowners failed to enforce beyond the statute of limitations (no action for more than 3 years).

 They are often more restrictive than zoning or planning restrictions. The sheriff's department, department of housing, planning and zoning will <u>NOT</u> hear complaints about non-compliance with private use restrictions.

 The best course of action is to file a complaint to the HOA and then to take court action if the offending owner does not correct the issue. The homeowner or HOA sues for an INJUNCTION to achieve compliance.

- <u>Public Land Use Controls</u> – are public land use restrictions designed to promote the health, safety and welfare of the public. This is accomplished through the use of <u>Police Power</u> – which is the government's right to impose laws, including building codes and zoning ordinances. The government can place use restrictions such as the type of property to be built (residential, commercial, industrial, agricultural) – including the size and density. Each category has multiple categories; for example residential includes townhouses, condos, 1-4 unit dwellings, etc.
- Common zoning terms include:
  - <u>Building Codes</u> – a set of requirements that relate to the construction of buildings (fire control, plumbing, electrical and other safety matters).
  - <u>Variance</u> – a minor change or deviation from the normal zoning ordinance as a result of undue hardship that is not caused by the property owner. For example, a county establishes a 20 ft setback rather than the previous 15 ft setback resulting in the lot that a couple purchased no longer being considered buildable. A variance may be granted to *prevent economic* hardship, however is not granted to *maximize owner profit*.
  - <u>Non-conforming Use</u> – when an existing use is no longer approved under the new zoning laws. For example, a family has operated a convenience store or gas station for 50 years in an area without restriction. The Zoning changes to single family residential only. The convenience store or gas station is a <u>Legal Non-Conforming Use</u> that is 'grandfathered in'. The convenience store is allowed to continue operations and owners can transfer or sell the property with the right for it to continue. If operations cease, the legal non-conforming Use protection ends. A party that decides to reopen the convenience store or gas station would be considered an <u>Illegal Use</u> – a direct violation of the current zoning ordinance unless they are able to rezone.
  - <u>Special Use Permit</u> – sometimes called <u>Conditional Use Permit</u> – already provided for in the zoning ordinance. Typically determined as part of a long range development plan – where the municipality envisions growth in an area and has determined that a hospital, for example, will be needed to serve the community. They have not determined the exact location, however know that it should be in a general area. Through planning and zoning they establish the minimum criteria (# of beds, size of lot, services, etc.) and the general area in which the facility can be located. The first developer to meet the criteria will be

granted the special use permit without having to go through the ordinary rezoning process. Commonly used for churches, daycares, affordable housing, etc. **Also used to approve PUDs.**

➢ <u>Overlay District</u> – additional layer of rules or regulations that are added to a particular area (think of an old projector and transparency – if a map of the city is being projected and then an additional layer is added – outlining new rules). Commonly used for flood zones to limit improvements, aesthetics set minimum standards or historical zones to retain character.

➢ <u>Subdivision Regulations</u> – The definition of a subdivision is a tract of land divided into two or more lots. Subdivisions must be approved by city planning and zoning and city council as it can increase the costs to a municipality (for schools, trash removal, police protection, etc.). Prior to offering lots for sale, accepting a contract or earnest money, a broker must determine if the plat has <u>Preliminary Approval</u>. Purchasers cannot close on the lot until <u>Final Approval</u> has been obtained (final plat recorded). The buyer cannot close for *5 days* from final approval and may terminate the contract within *15 days* if the lot has materially changed from preliminary plat. The sale of lots in an unapproved subdivision can result in criminal penalties and action by the Real Estate Commission.

➢ The subdivision developer should complete the Owners Association Disclosure Addendum for Properties Exempt from the Residential Property Disclosure Statement to inform buyer about the existence of a homeowners association as well as the fees associated and services provided.

➢ <u>Road Maintenance Agreement</u> – NC law requires the disclosure of the party who is required to maintain the roads, which must be made in writing (although does not require a road maintenance agreement be established). A developer must state whether roads will be public or private. The mere fact that roads are built to NCDOT standards does not guarantee that roads will be "Public" (maintained by tax dollars). Roads must be <u>built</u> to standards, <u>dedicated</u> to NCDOT and then must be <u>accepted</u> by NCDOT. The listing broker should ensure that the seller provides disclosure as this is a material fact. The disclosure should be given prior to accepting an offer to purchase or payment of an earnest money deposit. It is the responsibility of the broker representing the buyer to ensure the buyer receives and signs the mandatory disclosure. A broker should obtain a copy of the road maintenance agreement, if applicable, to disclose the costs/terms to potential buyers and their lenders.

Questions:

o Can an owner of a property prevent condemnation?
o What happens when a property is taken through eminent domain when the property is subject to a lease agreement?
o A property owner would not have to go through the formal rezoning process if they qualify for a _____?
o Verizon files for bankruptcy protection. What happens to the easements that they own for cell towers?

- o Tony purchases a property that has an appurtenant easement to cross a neighbor's property. He has not visited his property for 5 years, thus has not used the easement. Can the owner of the servient deem the easement abandoned?

Liens – A security interest in a property where upon default the lender may force the sale to recover some or all of the proceeds lent. It is a form of encumbrance to property, but not the only encumbrance. Think of an encumbrance as a broad category (liens, encroachments, easements, restrictive covenants, etc.) and a lien as a financial obligation. Typically the first to record is the first to be paid – see mechanics liens and lien priority below for further details. Types of liens include:

- o <u>General Liens</u> – a lien against all property, real and personal, owned by a person.
  - ➢ Judgment – granted by the courts becomes a lien once recorded at the county courthouse. The lien should be attached in the county in which the property is located. Judgment liens in North Carolina are for 10 years unless re-recorded.
  - ➢ Income Tax Lien – whether state or federal. Often wrongly assumed to have the highest priority for payment (see lien priority below).
  - ➢ Personal Property Tax Lien – typically for cars or other taxed property owned.
- o <u>Specific Liens</u> – a lien against specific real property. Listed below in order of priority.
  - ➢ Real Property Taxes (also called Ad Valorem Tax) – highest priority lien that attaches on January 1, is payable September 1 and is late after January 5 of the following year. In NC the tax rate is per $100 of assessed value, where assessed value is the market value of the property on the revaluation date (revaluation is only required to occur every 8 years – octennial reappraisal – but may be done every year). The <u>Machinery Act</u> provides for real property taxation but **does NOT set the rate of taxation** (which is based on the municipalities tax base and budget requirements).
  - ➢ Special Assessment – may be public or private. Commonly charged for the installation of water and sewer lines, paving, sidewalks, street lights, etc. for public or replacement or maintenance of common area items if private through the HOA.
  - ➢ Mortgage – the IOU for the loan on a particular property that creates a specific lien. Interest is paid in arrears (June's payment is for May's interest).
  - ➢ Deed of Trust – a three party document (mortgagor/mortgagee/trustee) that creates the security interest in a <u>Title Theory</u> state allowing for non-judicial foreclosure (by advertisement). See the Finance Section for additional details.
  - ➢ Mechanics Lien – a special lien reserved for contractors or subcontractors that may jump in priority. The lien must be filed within 120 days from the last date of labor or materials and the contractor must sue to enforce the lien within 180 days from the last date of labor or materials. If this occurs then the contractor's lien will jump back to the first day labor or materials were provided (if the contractor does not meet the deadline – they lose the special treatment). There are additional rules in NC regarding the appointment of a lien agent for projects that require a permit and are over $30,000.

LIEN PRIORITY

- Costs of Sale (Foreclosure)
- Real Property Taxes and Public Assessments
- Liens in Order of Recordation (except for mechanics liens that can jump in priority as described above)

Transfer of Title to Real Property

- o Types of transfer:
  - ➢ Voluntary Alienation – transfer of property through sale or gift by deed.
  - ➢ Involuntary Alienation – forced loss of property through lien foreclosure, adverse possession, eminent domain or escheat.

    PROBATE – the formal process of distributing a deceased person's assets. NOTE: Tenancy by the Entirety and Joint Tenancy co-owner(s) do not have to go through probate in order to claim the title to the property. The survivor(s) retains ownership automatically.
  - ➢ Testate Succession – transfer of property by will (**devise** if real property, **bequest** if personal property). A holographic will is a will that has been entirely written by hand. Last Will and Testament = owner died testate…with a will.
  - ➢ Intestate Succession – property distributed according to law when a person dies without a will. The laws vary from state to state.
  - ➢ When property is inherited – the basis is increased to the market value at the time of death. When the property is sold gain or loss will be determined based upon this stepped up basis rather than the tax basis of the deceased.
- o Transfer by Deed – a written document that transfers interest in real property from the owner (Grantor) to the buyer (Grantee). The level of assurances or warranties provided are based on the type of deed that was used to transfer ownership.
  - ➢ Essential Elements of a Deed – Recall – I.G.P.W.E.D. - "I Get Paid With Every Deal". 1) In Writing, 2) Grantor Competent (and Grantee Identified) Legal Capacity – (age, sober, sale, and legal owner), 3) Property Adequately Described, 4) Words of Conveyance, 5) Execution - Signed by ALL Owners, and 6) Delivery and Acceptance.
  - ➢ Non-Essential Elements of a Deed – although you may be crazy not to – the deed does not have to be dated, witnessed, recorded, acknowledged / notarized, state sales price or be sealed (extends statute of limitations. A deed must be notarized in order to be recorded.

     Under the N.C. Connor Act – a deed must be recorded to protect against 3rd parties transfers. In order for a deed to be recorded it must be notarized. NC is a "race state" meaning that the first to record is generally has priority to the property. Contracts to convey real estate, options, deeds and deeds of trust, mortgages, leases exceeding 3 years, easements, restrictive covenants and assignments of real estate interests must be recorded to protect against claims from 3rd parties. Failure to record a deed creates an opportunity for another party to claim interest. Since the deed is not recorded, the new buyer does not have constructive notice that the property had changed hands. Should this happen, the party that records will have a greater claim to the property. The party that failed to record will hold

a *valid* deed, however it will no longer be *enforceable*. In the event of dispute over ownership a suit to quiet title would determine the party with the greater claim to the property.

 When a seller commits fraud and sells the same property to multiple buyers, the first to record will have superior title. While all deeds may be valid (I.G.P.W.E.D.), only the recorded deed will be enforceable.

 The <u>Torrens System</u> is a method of protecting property from adverse possession claims by registering it (similar to vehicle registration). Property transfers must be noted on the Torrens Certificate to be valid. The courts are involved in the transfer.

Deeds

o A deed is used to transfer ownership of a property from the owner/grantor and the receiver/grantee. A deed does not prove or guarantee ownership. It is important to know the various types of deeds and the covenants contained, if any.

o Types of Deeds:

> General Warranty Deed/Full Covenant – The best and most desirable deed in North Carolina where the grantor warrants to defend the title forever providing the grantee with the most protection. Includes the covenant of seisin – grantor has the right to convey; covenant of quiet enjoyment – new owner will not be disturbed by claims; covenant against encumbrances – other than those disclosed and assumed; covenant of further assurance – grantor will cooperate in signing additional documents; and a warranty forever. The Standard NCAR/NCBA Offer to Purchase states the seller will provide this type of deed.

> Special Warranty Deed – Limited warranty deed that is typically used in foreclosure (however some banks are moving to Quitclaim Deeds). This deed warrants against defects that occurred during the period of time that the Grantor owned the property, however does not warrant anything that occurred prior.

> Quitclaim Deed – Without warranty and often used to correct an issue or remove a <u>cloud from the title</u>. Typically a deed of release where the party signing gives up (<u>or quits</u>) any interest that they may have in the property. The grantor makes no warranty and has no obligation to defend the title.

> Bargain and Sale Deed – Equivalent to a quitclaim deed except that the grantor implies ownership of the property being conveyed. This deed is not used in North Carolina, however is used in other states.

 The type of deed does <u>not</u> guarantee that it provides <u>Marketable Title</u> - free of liens and encumbrances (which may affect the transfer, since an unsatisfied lien - other than in a foreclosure, will transfer to the new owner).

 You are more likely to see questions related to the general warranty, special warranty and quitclaim deeds.

Habendum Clause is typically used as a distractor – it is the clause in a deed or lease that defines the type of interest and rights to be enjoyed (typically defining limitations). In addition, the Covenant of Seisin is often used as a distractor.

   ➢ Special Purpose Deeds – Timber deed – the right to harvest trees; Mineral deed – transfer of mineral rights; Trustee deed – granted to Trustee upon foreclosure sale involving a Deed of Trust; Sheriff's deed – granted upon sale of property to satisfy a judgment; Tax deed – granted at a tax foreclosure sale; Deed of Gift – must be recorded within 2 years or is invalid and no warranty no matter how transferred.

o Excise Tax – may be referred to as Revenue or Deed Stamps. Tax paid by the Seller when real property is sold in North Carolina, affixed to the first page of the deed. It is charged at $1 per $50 of the sales price, rounded up to the nearest dollar. The deed cannot be recorded unless it shows the excise tax has been paid.
   ➢ Excise Tax = [Sales Price / 500] round up (tax man is greedy)

Title Assurance – Defined as the examination of recorded documents to determine if a seller can deliver marketable title to the buyer. The attorney provides an opinion and this is the basis for whether a Title Insurance Company will write a policy that will protect the bank and/or buyer.
o The attorney performs a Title Search using public records located at the Register of Deeds office the County in which the property is located.
o The Chain of Title details all conveyances and encumbrances affecting the title over a period of time. For practical purposes attorneys typically go back 30 to 60 years.
o An Abstract of Title is a condensed history of the title – a summary of all recorded documents.
o Only an attorney can provide an Opinion of Title which is used to determine if insurable marketable title exists (free of liens, judgments, taxes and encumbrances that would affect the transfer of the property).

o Methods of Clearing Clouds on Title
   ➢ Quitclaim deed – quit whatever claim a party may have, if any.
   ➢ Suit to Quiet Title – court action to determine ownership – often used in adverse possession claims however can be used in foreclosure actions or any actions seeking to prove superior claim of title to a property.
   ➢ Marketable Title Act – the extinguishment of all claims or defects dating beyond 30 years. For example, a mortgage without a corresponding satisfaction of lien recorded that is greater than 30 years from maturity.

Title Insurance – Defined as an insurance policy with two types – one for the owner and one for the lender, that covers losses that may occur as a result of a defect in the title. It is an **indemnity policy** where the owner is reimbursed or compensated due to a title defect or claim. A Standard Policy protects against issues with the public record (forgery, duress, etc). An Extended Policy protects against issues that are not a matter of public record (encroachments – as long as buyer has updated survey, adverse possession, etc.). The buyer pays the premium once – at closing for both the lender and owner policies, so there are no renewal premiums.

Does it end?

- o Owner Policy – protects against claims arising from past activity up to the original purchase price of the property.
- o Lender Policy – protects the lender up to the mortgage balance (coverage decreases as the principal balance decreases). Typically paid for by the borrower and a requirement for all federally related mortgage loans.

   Title Insurance only protects acts from the past – events that happened before new buyer purchased the property. Will not cover issues that buyer causes after closing.

   In order to have "full coverage" for both title defects as well as encroachments the buyer must purchase a survey. The borrower will pay the cost of both the lender and owner's policy.

pes of Real Property Description

- o Metes and Bounds – The most common method used in North Carolina to describe property, that often references monuments and is commonly found as part of the recorded <u>Deed</u>. A monument is a visible marker used to establish the boundaries of a property. The survey begins at the Point of Beginning (POB) and the final call must end back at the POB and **must be measured clockwise.** Property lines are typically marked with cement markers or iron stakes driven into the ground. The description provides the degree of angle, direction and distance between each point. **This is the dominant method of describing properties in both deeds and contracts in North Carolina, noting that the standard contract used by REALTORS does not provide for it – brokers reference recorded documents (deed book + page, plat book + page, PIN / PID, Lot + Block, and other legal description).**

   Imperfect – When the survey fails to end back at the point of beginning.

   When a monument is destroyed (tree, barn, etc.) it does not invalidate a survey as other points of reference are included for a surveyor to determine its location.

- o Government Rectangular Survey System – Typically used by states that were not a part of the original 13 colonies. It is a grid system developed by the US Government that references meridians and ranges that run north/south and baselines and tiers that run east/west.
  - ➤ There are 36 sections in a township and it is displayed as a 6 x 6 grid. Section 1 is at the top right hand corner and the sections snake from left to right, ending with Section 36 at the bottom right corner of the grid.
  - ➤ Each section is 1 mile by 1 mile and contains 640 acres. 1 mile is 5,280 linear feet. 1 acre is 43,560 square feet.
  - ➤ When reading the description you start from the right and read toward the left.
  - ➤ The <u>baseline</u> runs east to west. The <u>principal meridian</u> runs north to south.

- o Reference to a Recorded Document – This is the most common method used when completing the Standard NCAR/NCBA Offer to Purchase and Contract. Licensees reference documents that have been recorded at the courthouse. Reference is made to a recorded Plat Book + Page, reference to recorded deed by Deed Book + Page, PIN / PID and other legal description.

 Informal reference to the street and house number is not considered legally sufficie identification. It is common practice to include this information in addition to references to recorded documents when completing the OPC.

Questions:

- How can a deed be valid but unenforceable?
- What is the covenant of seisin?
- What is a habendum clause?
- _____ protects an owner against claims that are not a matter of public record?
- What is indemnity?

AGENCY

Agency – 3 Categories
- Universal Agency – All-encompassing powers to do anything that a principal could do. Usually granted through a Power of Attorney and may be referred to as an Attorney-in-Fact **(where you stand in for the party and can sign on his/her behalf).**
- General Agency – Broad range of authority related to a very specific or defined task. This is the typical relationship between an agent and his/her <u>brokerage</u> and occurs in property managemer between the agent and the principal. **(Property Management / Affiliation with a Brokerage)**
- Special Agency – Typically has one narrow defined task. Commonly the relationship between an agent and the <u>seller, buyer or tenant</u>. The agent acts as an information gatherer to assist the principal in making their decision.   The Special Agent has no authority to bind the principal to a transaction. **(Representing Buyer / Seller / Tenant)**

Brokers

- A Broker / Provisional Broker is typically an **<u>independent contractor</u>** – sets hours, no taxes are withheld, typically no benefits and the broker will have to pay income and payroll taxes based upon his/her profit. The Broker also pays the costs associated with the business (marketing, ce phone, MLS access, Errors & Omissions insurance, etc). Income is reported on IRS form 1099. A **<u>employee</u>** would receive a W-2, have defined hours and less control over when work is perform and the Firm would need to contribute his/her share of the payroll taxes.
- A broker acts as a General Agent with his/her brokerage, with a limited ability to bind the firm t agreements and will act as a Special Agent with buyers and sellers, where they lack the ability to sign on behalf of his/her client.

Agency and Common Law
- Common Law – is the body of law that governs the relationship between the principal/client and the agent.

- Duties Owed to Principal – O.L.D. C.A.R. – Obedience, Loyalty, Disclosure, Confidentiality, Accounting and Reasonable Skill /Care /Diligence
    - Obedience – agent must follow the principal's lawful instructions.
    - Loyalty – agent must place the client's interest above all others, including their own.
    - Disclosure - agent must disclose material facts to all parties involved in a transaction. The agent must disclose personal/confidential information obtained about the other party to the contract (unless acting as dual agent). In addition they are required to present all offers, both written and oral.
    - Confidentiality - An agent cannot disclose personal or confidential information that would weaken their client's bargaining position (unless it is a material fact).
    - Accounting – for all funds handled (EMD, DDF, and Security Deposit) as well as safeguarding the property.
    - Reasonable Diligence, Skill, Care – agent must be competent and knowledgeable about the type of real estate being sold, leased or exchanged and the area in which the property is physically located.

- Duties Owed to 3rd Party Customers – H.F.D. – Honest, Fairness, Disclosure of Material Facts
- Duties the Principal Owes the Firm – Good Faith (cooperation, truthfulness) and Compensation.
- In the event that a Principal Seller refuses to pay the commission that has been earned by the agent(s), the attorney or firm cannot prevent closing and should never advise the Buyer not to honor the contract. Remember that we typically have 3 contracts in play – 1) Offer to Purchase and Contract between the Buyer and Seller; 2) Listing Agreement between the Seller's Agent and Seller; and 3) The Buyer Agency Agreement between the Buyer's Agent and Buyer. If the Buyer were to breach his/her contract with the Seller, the Seller would be entitled to liquidated damages (retain DDF and entitled to EMD as sole and exclusive remedy for breach under the Standard NCAR/NCBA Offer to Purchase). The agent should refer his/her client to an attorney if the client wants to breach the contract. The agent should never state that the seller or buyer "must" honor all contract. The non-breaching party is entitled to remedies and buyer or seller may be subject to a lawsuit to recover the commission, legal expenses and interest, compensatory damages on behalf of the buyer or specific performance.
- Vicarious Liability - The Principal can be held liable for civil damages for the actions of their agent (tort) in the event the agent breaches duties to a third party. It is possible if the wrongful act is severe enough, that the Principal may be subject to criminal prosecution if the breach rises to the level of a violation of a criminal statute.

 The Principal is the party that contracts with the Firm to represent them (Seller – Listing Agreement, Buyer – Buyer Agency Agreement, Landlord – Property Management Agreement, or Tenant – Tenant Representation Agreement).

 There can be confusion about <u>Obedience</u>. We must follow our client's lawful instructions. Under North Carolina License Law and Commission Rules we must present all offers and a seller cannot relieve us of that responsibility. In addition a seller cannot direct us to disclose a buyer's offer to another as we cannot do this

without the express permission of the buyer that made the offer. The client cannot require that we omit a material fact, discriminate against a buyer or seller, or ask us to discriminate on the client's behalf.

 The agency agreement is owned by the FIRM. What happens if the broker leaves? Can the broker take the listing?

- o The brokerage (agency) agreement establishes the relationship and the scope of the agent's authority to act on behalf of the principal. All written agreements must define the firm's duties to the principal.
- o Agency agreements are between the Principal (Client) and the Firm.

Agreements That Must Be In Writing from Inception (at the start)
- o Listing Agreements
- o Property Management Agreements
- o Any agreement that seeks EXCLUSIVITY or contains a definite end date.

 Written agreements must have a definite end date (property management agreements can have automatic renewal).

 Must contain Non-Discriminatory language and the licensee's license number.

 Standard forms must meet Commission requirements but the forms are _not_ written or approved by the Commission.

Agreements That Can Be Oral at Inception:
- o Buyer Agency Agreements
- o Tenant Representation Agreements

 Non-Exclusive...we can see other people. Open Ended...no end date.

 Must be reduced to writing prior to the preparation of an offer to buy or rent.

Common Forms of Agency Relationships
> Exclusive Buyer / Seller Agency – may be referred to as exclusive or **_Single Agency_**.

- o Exclusive Seller Agency – where the firm represents only the Seller. Each agent within the office becomes a Subagent to the Seller and cannot represent a Buyer in the transaction.
  - ➢ Agent owes all of their loyalty and obedience to the Seller (so long as they comply with license and common law duties).
  - ➢ Historically all agents worked for the Seller as they typically paid the listing agent and the agent that brought the buyer.

 If a Seller's Agent learns of personal or confidential information about the Buyer they have an obligation to disclose this information to the Seller (the buyer's ability or willingness to pay more for the home). In addition we owe confidentiality regarding information about our Seller. For example the Seller's Agent cannot disclose that a

Seller will take less than the asking price or that the Seller is currently delinquent on their mortgage (unless foreclosure notice has been sent).

 If a buyer <u>customer</u> seeks guidance about restrictive or protective covenants and whether an activity or action is permitted, you can provide them with a copy of the covenants, however since the broker represents the SELLER, the broker cannot help them determine if the property will meet their needs. The broker will need to refer them to an Attorney.

o Exclusive Buyer Agency – where the firm represents only the Buyer and cannot represent the Seller in the transaction. An Exclusive Right to Represent Buyer agreement would require a buyer to pay commission no matter how they are introduced to the property they purchase.
  ➤ Agent owes all of their loyalty and obedience to the Buyer (as long as they comply with license and common law duties).

     If a Buyer's Agent learns of personal or confidential information about the Seller they have an obligation to disclose this information to the Buyer. The Buyer's Agent also owes their client confidentiality and should not disclose information that would weaken his/her bargaining position, unless it rises to the level of a material fact.

o Dual Agency – Occurs when the firm, that practices dual agency, has an agency agreement with both the Buyer and the Seller and they have expressly agreed to dual agency representation. There is a <u>slight reduction</u> in what an agent is permitted to perform. The Agent(s) must treat both parties fairly and equally by not advocating for one party over another – cannot discuss matters relating to price or terms of sale other than those offered. Dual agents cannot pass personal or confidential information about one party to the other unless it rises to the level of material fact. They can prepare a Comparative Market Analysis with a probable sales price range, but cannot tell a Buyer what to offer or a Seller what to accept.
  ➤ If agreed to by the Seller at the time that they sign the Listing Agreement, then must be in writing.
  ➤ If agreed to by the Buyer, then oral agreement is permitted while the Buyer Agency Agreement is oral. Must be reduced to writing prior to the preparation of an offer.
  ➤ If dual agency is agreed to at a later date, then the <u>determination of when it must be in writing is dictated by the Buyer agency agreement</u>. The Seller can orally agree to dual agency if the Buyer Agency Agreement is oral. If the Buyer Agency Agreement is in writing, then the seller authorization of dual agency must be in writing.
  ➤ Undisclosed Dual Agency is illegal (working for both the buyer and seller without consent of both parties).
o Designated Agency – is a form of dual agency – can't have designated agency without dual agency. The Principal must authorize both dual and designated agency and the firm must offer designated agency representation. When permitted the agents can return to their traditional advocacy roles similar to exclusive seller and exclusive buyer representation. The firm must have a written policy to perform designated agency.

- The designated agents are appointed by the Broker-in-Charge and the agent's <u>cannot</u> have personal or confidential information at the time of appointment that would weaken the bargaining position of the other party.
- Designated agency <u>cannot</u> be practiced between the Broker-in-Charge and a Provisional Broker under his/her supervision.

 Which type of agency affords a client with greater representation – dual or designated?

Agency Disclosure

o <u>Agent to Potential Client / Customer</u> - In a real estate transaction, whether residential or commercial, it is paramount for all parties to know how they will be working together. In fact under North Carolina License Law a licensee is forbidden to provide brokerage services until agency has been determined. Agents are required to review the **Working with Real Estate Agents Brochure** at <u>First Substantial Contact</u> (FSC). FSC can occur in person, over the phone or electronically. It is the point in time that the discussion shifts from facts about the property to the buyer's needs or desires and financial ability to complete a purchase.
- Open House – An agent is not required to immediately provide the Working with Real Estate Agents brochure when a prospective purchaser enters the home. Only when the conversation shifts. Refer to the definition of FSC above.
- The Working with Real Estate Agents brochure is <u>NOT</u> a contract.
- The prospective client or customer is not obligated to sign the form unless they are acknowledging Seller Subagency representation. If a prospective client or customer refuses initial or sign the form, the broker should note it on the form and retain a copy in his/her records for the prescribed time period (3 years from the date of last activity).

o <u>Buyers Agent to Seller or Sellers Agent</u> – A buyer's agent must disclose their agency status to the seller or seller's agent upon <u>Initial Contact</u>. Initial Contact can occur when gathering information about the property or may occur as late as the presentation of an offer. Students sometimes confuse Initial Contact and First Substantial Contact.

Disclosure of Facts

o Material Fact – a fact that would affect the buyer's decision to buy or the seller's decision to sell. Some examples include a leaky roof or other condition related to the property (such as zoning change or roads may be widened, issues related to drainage or perk problems).

o An agent is responsible to disclose things that they <u>know or reasonably should have known</u>. Failure to disclose or providing false information falls under the following categories:
- Willful – Agent acted with <u>intent</u> to purposefully lie or withhold information. The act of purposefully not seeking additional information about something that is a material fact would also fall under this category.
- Negligent – Agent made an error about something that they reasonably should have known. Forgetting about something that the seller has disclosed would fall into this category.
- Misrepresentation – Agent tells a lie. They have said something and it is wrong. **Opened Mouth.**
- Omission – The Agent fails to tell the customer/client something. **Did not Open Mouth.**

A Seller tells the listing agent that there is a foundation issue but instructs the agent not to disclose. If the agent complies what are they guilty of, if anything?

 An agent that provides their client with outdated covenants, which are relied upon by the client, would be guilty of negligent misrepresentation.

 What would an agent be guilty of if they fail to disclose the existence of restrictive/protective covenants, since the subdivision was located outside of their normal selling area and they were therefore unaware?

o Some states require full disclosure from the seller of any material facts for which they are aware, which conflicts with North Carolina's caveat emptor – let the buyer beware. A seller in North Carolina is not obligated to disclose many items; the responsibility falls on the agent to disclose or the buyer to discover issues through his/her investigation of the property.
  ➢ The N.C. General Assembly has determined that certain items are material facts that must be disclosed – meth labs, leaking polybutylene plumbing – even if repaired or replaced, and synthetic stucco (EIFS) – even if totally replaced.
  ➢ Some items in North Carolina are <u>not</u> a material fact – such as the presence of mold (unless extreme), the fact that a sex offender lives in or near the property, that the property is stigmatized (death, suicide or violent crime) or that the house is haunted.
  ➢ An agent cannot disclose if the current or previous occupants had HIV or AIDS as this is a protected class under State and Federal Fair Housing (Handicap).
  ➢ Latent Defect – hidden. Not easily discoverable. An agent should always encourage a buyer to obtain an inspection before purchasing a property. Unless an agent is aware of a latent defect (the seller disclosed it), it would not be reasonable for a prudent agent to discover the problem. A broker is not liable for failing to disclose a latent defect. A broker that is aware of a defect and fails to disclose the fact is guilty of willful omission.
  ➢ Patent Defect – plain as day – easily discoverable. An agent that fails to disclose a patent defect may be liable to the client/customer in civil court and may face disciplinary action from the Commission.
o Puffing – stating something that is exaggerated or that is subjective and not easily verifiable. For example an agent states in an ad that "This is the best house in Durham". Some prospective buyers may agree and other may feel it is the best house to knock down. This is a statement of opinion and would not be considered misrepresentation.

:ting Agreements
o Types of Agreements:
  ➢ Open/<u>Non-Exclusive</u> Listing – Agent vs. Other Agents and the Seller – The agent is in competition with the Seller and any other agent that the Seller contracts with. The agent that brings the buyer is compensated unless the seller finds the buyer and then no commission is due. An agent that is not party to the open listing is not entitled to compensation from the seller if they bring a buyer.

- Exclusive Agency Listing Agreement – Agent vs. Seller – The agent is no longer competing with other agents, however is still in competition with the Seller. If the Seller locates the buyer then no commission is due. The agent that is party to the agreement must be procuring cause to receive compensation.
- Exclusive Right to Sell Listing Agreement – This listing agreement provides the most protection to the Firm. No matter how the property is sold the firm is guaranteed the commission that was agreed to in the contract. It does not matter who procures the buyer – the agent, a buyer's agent or the seller. **This is the most common form used in North Carolina.**
- Limited Service Agreement – an agreement where the Seller can negotiate the level of service that will be provided, similar to ordering À la carte. Sellers can select to list the property in the MLS, have the broker negotiate the transaction, advertise, hold open houses, etc. This is typically for a flat or reduced fee. It is important to remember that an agent can contractually reduce the services that will be performed, however that does not limit or waive the duties under North Carolina License Law (disclosure of material facts, avoiding false promises, negligent/willful misrepresentation, etc.).

Compensation

- All compensation is negotiable. Compensation rates are not set by the Real Estate Commission, MLS or REALTOR Associations.
- Under the Sherman Antitrust Act a brokerage can set its own commission rate, provide guidance to affiliated brokers about the fee to charge and empower an affiliated broker to negotiate within set parameters. In addition they cannot boycott a lender, attorney, inspector or other real estate firm. Fines for violation can range from $100,000 and three years in prison for an individual and up to $1 million for a corporation/brokerage.
- Commission is earned when an agent procures a ready, willing and able buyer on price and terms outlined in the listing agreement or upon terms that are acceptable to the Seller (entering into a contract).
- The Firm is entitled to a commission even if the transaction does not close (seller or spouse refuses to sign, buyer and seller agree to terminate, there is a defect in title, buyer terminates the contract, seller refused to negotiate with a buyer based on a protected class under federal fair housing). It is **important to know when compensation is earned when the transaction fails.**
- Procuring Cause – the firm that originates a series of events without a break in continuity resulting in a ready, willing and able buyer purchasing the property on the Seller's terms or those agreed to by the parties. In North Carolina the listing agreement must be in writing from inception and the buyer agency agreement must be reduced to writing prior to writing an offer or the Firm waives the right to claim compensation.

Solicitation / Marketing to Prospective Clients

- Laws affecting Solicitation:
  - Do Not Call – Broker can't call someone that has registered on the list unless they have a prior business relationship within the past 18 months or the broker is granted permission to call.
  - Do Not Fax – Can't send unsolicited faxes. Must contain a prominent opt out provision.
  - Can-Spam – Must provide an opt-out so that a customer/client can elect not to receive future email solicitations.

- ➤ REALTOR® Code of Ethics – A realtor cannot solicit other realtor's clients, tortuous interference of contract, and may be subject to civil liability. Recommended that you include "if your home is currently listed, please disregard" in all mailings to avoid violation.

   Note that "snail" mail is not restricted above. Agents have no restrictions on solicitation by regular mail.

- o Common Provisions in a Listing Agreement
    - ➤ Adequate Property Description – referencing previously recorded documents (recall that the address alone is not sufficient – better to reference deed book and page, plat book and page and other legal information).
    - ➤ Price and Terms of Sale – will the Seller accept cash offers, conventional, FHA/VA financing, provide seller financing or assumption. A broker should caution a seller from accepting an offer with FHA/VA financing when a property requires repairs and the seller lacks the funds to complete them.
    - ➤ Expiration Date – the listing agreement must have a definite end date where it terminates without prior notice. You cannot agree to list a property "until it sells". Automatic extensions in a listing agreement are not allowed under North Carolina Commission Rules.
    - ➤ Non-discrimination language – **THE AGENT (FIRM) SHALL CONDUCT ALL BROKERAGE ACTIVITIES IN REGARD TO THIS AGREEMENT WITHOUT THE RESPECT OF THE RACE, COLOR, SEX, NATIONAL ORIGIN, HANDICAP OR FAMILIAL STATUS OF ANY PARTY OR PROSPECTIVE PARTY TO THE AGREEMENT.**
    - ➤ Licensee's License Number
    - ➤ Agency Relationship – authorization of dual and/or designated agency or desire for exclusive representation.
    - ➤ Brokerage Fee – commission percentage, flat fee or other method. There is no "usual" or "customary" fee as it would be a violation of the Sherman Anti-Trust Act (no price fixing / no boycotting). Note that net listings are legal however are discouraged. A net listing is where the firm keeps any money in excess of an agreed upon amount the seller needs.
    - ➤ Cooperation with Other Firms – addresses how a buyer's agent or subagent may be compensated or if compensation will be offered.
    - ➤ Firm's and Seller's Duties
    - ➤ Protection Period – when the agreement terminates, the agent(s) are protected for a certain period of time. Should a party decide to purchase the home that was introduced during the listing period and within an agreed period of time, then the broker will be entitled to receive compensation under certain circumstances. Note that entering into a representation agreement with another agent typically terminates the protection period.
- o Termination of Listing Agreements:
    - ➤ Full Performance – the property is sold!!
    - ➤ Death of the owner or an independent broker (working alone)
    - ➤ Destruction of the property – (with damage the buyer may elect to close and receive the insurance proceeds for repair)
    - ➤ Breach of Contract (broker may be entitled to compensation)
    - ➤ The Brokerage Firm ceases operations.

A listing agreement does not terminate if a Provisional Broker (salesperson) dies or is declared insane as the listing is with the FIRM and not the agent. The brokerage can appoint another agent to fulfill the firms duties.

- o   If a provisional broker / broker is a member of the MLS, they should complete a "property data sheet" that details information to be included in the listing which is then shared with other agents and the public.
- o   Remember that a licensee must provide accurate information to avoid willful/negligent misrepresentation/omission as they could face civil liability through the courts and/or action taken against his/her license by the Commission (reprimand/censure/suspend/revoke).
- o   Square Footage – the North Carolina Real Estate Commission (NCREC) does not require an agent to disclose the square footage of a building, however many MLS's do require this information. If an agent discloses the square footage it must be accurate. The listing agent is primarily responsible; however a buyer's agent may be held responsible if a reasonable agent could identify the error. The agent remains liable even when they hire a specialist to measure the home.
  - ➢   Square Footage is reported as Living Area and Other Area and commonly reported broken down for above and below grade. Under the NCREC **Residential Square Footage Guidelines** agents should use outside measurements whenever possible. When not possible, agents may take interior measurements then add 6 inches to any outside wall.
  - ➢   <u>H</u>appy <u>F</u>eet <u>D</u>ance <u>A</u>lways – How to remember the definition of <u>Living Area</u> in North Carolina <u>H</u>eated, <u>F</u>inished, and <u>D</u>irectly <u>A</u>ccessible. Additionally the ceiling height must be 7ft (6ft 4in under ducts or beams) and if the ceiling is sloped – 50% or more must be 7 ft or greater and if so can include down to where the ceiling height is 5 ft.
  - ➢   Garages, porches and unfinished areas are not included in the <u>living area</u>.
  - ➢   Townhouse – take inside measurements then add 6 inches for any exterior or party wall.
  - ➢   Condo – only take inside measurements as you only own your airspace. Do not add 6 inches.
  - ➢   You may need to determine the square footage of various shapes – rectangles, squares and triangles. Note that the square footage of a square or rectangle is calculated by multiplying the length by the width. A triangle = ½ base times height.

 Note HEATED square footage is included in living area...there is no requirement for <u>air conditioning</u>. Do not include garages, decks, carports, etc. in the living area calculation.

- o   Residential Property Disclosure Statement – as the name implies it is for <u>residential sales</u> (1-4 units) whether the property is listed with a broker or offered for sale by the owner. The seller completes the form <u>NOT the agent</u>. The seller can select Yes, No or No Representation for each question on the form which addresses specific questions about the property and seeks disclosure of problems or defects. The Seller is not obligated to disclose anything (we are a **Caveat Emptor** state meaning "let the Buyer beware"); this includes items that may be considered material facts. There are exemptions from the use of the form for new construction, foreclosure, transfers among family and transactions where the buyer is already occupying the residential dwelling. For property being sold in a new subdivision with a HOA, the developer should complete the Owner

Association Disclosure and Addendum for Properties Exempt for the Property Disclosure Statement.

 Even if a Seller selects "No Representation" it does not relieve the agent of the responsibility to "Discover and Disclose" material facts. The seller is not obligated to disclose a known defect and will not be liable unless they have concealed the defect or tried to conceal it (fraud).

 If a Seller fails to deliver the form or provides it after contract, the buyer will have a rescission period – the earliest of 3 calendar days from the date of receipt, 3 calendar days from the date of contract or closing.

sic Contract Law

o A <u>Contract</u> is defined as an agreement between 2 or more parties to perform a legal act. The essential elements of a contract:
  - ➤ Mutual Assent / Voluntary Consent / Reality of Consent – there have been a meeting of the minds and mutual agreement of the parties without duress or undue influence. If there is a mistake or fraud / misrepresentation – the agreement may become void or voidable.
  - ➤ Consideration – something of value has been exchanged, however does not need to be money. The mutual promises in a bilateral agreement are sufficient to form a legally binding contract.
  - ➤ Capacity of the Parties –Mental incompetence can result when an individual is legally insane or intoxicated. Contracts with minors or someone that is intoxicated are <u>voidable</u> while contracts with someone declared insane are void. The minor can enforce the contract, however can elect not to purchase without consequence and may be able to rescind the contract even after reaching the age of majority (18) in some states.
  - ➤ Lawful Objective – lawful purpose to the contract.
o A guardian can be appointed to handle the affairs of minors. In the event a guardian can no longer perform, a new guardian must be appointed by the courts. The minor's school principal cannot sign on his/her behalf.

if sold to minor is it voidable by seller OR Buyer?

mmon Contract Terminology

  - ➤ Contracts can be <u>Express</u> – agreed to in writing or orally, <u>Implied</u> – born out of the actions of the parties, **Unilateral** – binding only if another party acts, or **Bilateral** – based on mutual promises between two parties (most real estate contracts).
  - ➤ Our ultimate goal is to form a <u>Valid</u> contract – an agreement that is legally enforceable.
  - ➤ Contracts can be <u>Voidable</u> – a contract that appears to be valid, however one party has the right to terminate (often due to breach, sale to a minor, damage to the property, fraud or misrepresentation).
  - ➤ A contract is <u>Void</u> –not legally enforceable (contract with someone that has been declared legally insane). Oddly, a void contract can be executed (see below) as long as it is <u>not</u> <u>disaffirmed</u> and in the event <u>both parties elect to perform</u>.
  - ➤ An <u>Executed</u> contract is one where all the terms have been legally performed in full.
  - ➤ An <u>Executory</u> contract is one that has not been fully performed.

- ➢ <u>Execute</u> means to sign and is commonly used as a distractor.
- ○ Uniform Electronic Transaction Act (UETA) – states that an electronic signature or contracts created via email, fax or other electronic means are legally binding and enforceable. Clients must agree to conduct the transaction electronically. The agreements are legally binding without delay – there is no time period required by law.
- ○ Termination of Contracts Occurs:
  - ➢ Full Performance
  - ➢ By Agreement Between the Parties – release, modification of the agreement, or <u>novation</u> – the substitution of a new contract for the previous one.
  - ➢ Operation of Law – bankruptcy of one of the parties / statute of limitations
  - ➢ Impossibility of Performance – destruction of the property, death or insanity of an independent broker – service contract (for listing and buyer agency)
- ○ Assignment – is generally allowed unless otherwise provided for in the contract. Note: The Standard NCAR/NCBA Offer to Purchase and Contract is assignable only with the express written permission of all parties or if either party is seeking to complete a <u>1031 Like Kind Exchange</u>.
- ○ Some Agreements Must Be in Writing – under the <u>Statute of Frauds</u> certain agreements must be in writing to be enforceable. Examples include a contract for the sale or transfer of real estate, lease agreement that exceed 3 years, non-compete agreements and option agreements. Some agreements are required to be in writing from inception under Commission Rule.

 The Parole Evidence Rule states that oral agreements are not binding and that any handwritten or added language that conflicts with the preprinted form overrides the preprinted form.

 What happens if a party was sane when they entered a contract and then subsequent to signing becomes insane? Is the contract binding? Yes. They did not lack capacity when they signed the agreement. What happens if a party goes insane subsequent to the purchase of a property? Can they void the contract and seek the return of their purchase money? No. They did not lack capacity when they closed on the property.

- ○ Remedies Upon Breach:
  - ➢ <u>Liquidated Damages</u> – Amount that is specified in advance in the contract. The amount must be reasonable. Under the Standard NCAR/NCBA Offer to Purchase and Contract the Earnest Money Deposit and Due Diligence Fee are liquidated damages in the event of breach by Buyer.
  - ➢ <u>Compensatory Damages</u> – Monetary damages based on actual loss in an amount that is necessary to "make the party whole". This is not meant to punish the party that breached the contract.
  - ➢ <u>Specific Performance</u> – In the event of a breach by Seller and the subject matter of the contract is not readily available from another source. In real estate contracts all real property is considered <u>unique</u> and therefore the buyer may be successful in forcing the sale.
  - ➢ <u>Rescission</u> – Termination of the contract when it can be proved that there was not meeting of the minds / reality of consent.

Questions:

o When would a seller not be liable to pay a commission to a broker upon the sale of his/her property to a buyer?

o What are the differences between execute, executory, and executed?

o Would a seller that discovers they have contracted with a minor be allowed to void the contract?

o What are the essential elements of a deed? A contract?

o Would an agent be responsible/liable for failing to disclose an issue such as standing water in the crawlspace during spring time, when the listing is taken in the fall and no evidence of past standing water is evident?

OFFER TO PURCHASE AND CONTRACT

o Brokers should utilize the Standard NCAR / NCBA Offer to Purchase and Contract (OPC) for residential sales (single family, 1-4 unit dwelling, condo or townhouse) or <u>use a form prepared by an attorney</u>. **BROKERS CANNOT DRAFT contracts or provisions to a contract. The Commission makes rules regarding standard forms, however does not approve forms for use.**

o Major Provisions of the Standard NCAR/NCBA OPC – North Carolina Form:

➢ Sales Price and Method of Payment

➢ Adequate Property Description

Refridge

➢ Provision for Fixtures that do not convey and will be retained by Seller or Personal Property that will be transferred to the Buyer – NOTE: if fixtures are not excepted in the contract the seller is obligated to leave them for the buyer. If personal property is not included in a contract then seller is not obligated to leave them for the buyer.

➢ Due Diligence – the period of time that a buyer has to investigate a property (inspection, survey, appraisal), apply for financing, and negotiate repairs. The period of time is referred to as the Due Diligence Period (DDP). During this period the Buyer may terminate the contract for <u>any reason or no reason</u> at all (it's raining outside...terminate). The DDP is "time is of the essence" meaning a drop dead date – if the buyer does not terminate by 5:00 p.m. on that date, the earnest money deposit will no longer be refundable in the event of termination or breach.

➢ Due diligence is very similar to an option agreement. The buyer has the option to opt out of the contract without additional penalty, other that the due diligence fee paid. In an option agreement, the optionee can decide to opt into the contract.

➢ Due Diligence Fee – an agreed upon amount, if any, for the right to perform due diligence. It is not required to form a legally binding contract, is <u>not refundable</u> (unless the Seller breaches), and is credited to the Buyer at closing.

➢ Earnest Money Deposit (EMD) – although not required to form a legally binding contract, it is money deposited with an escrow agent to demonstrate that the buyer is acting in good faith. The contract details how EMD will be treated:

• Credited to buyer upon closing

• Refunded upon termination of contract prior to the expiration of the Due Diligence Period – Buyer must provide written notice by 5:00 P.M.

- It is part of the <u>liquidated damages</u> that the Seller will receive in the event of breach of contract by buyer (the Seller's sole and exclusive remedy for Buyer's breach – EMD and DDF).
- Must be refunded if the Seller breaches the contract.

 Failure to deliver the EMD or DDF or if either payment is returned for insufficient funds by the bank does not automatically terminate a contract. The Seller must make demand and the Buyer then has <u>1 Banking Day</u> to provide good funds.

 What happens if the buyer signs a promissory note for the EMD? Is this part of the mortgage?

➤ Settlement / Closing Date – Settlement is when paperwork is signed. Closing is when the title record is updated and the bank provides a funding number to release funds. Settlement = Signing. Closing = Cash and keys.

 Closing is NOT "time is of the essence". Either party may delay for 14 days as long as they are making best efforts. The contract does not automatically terminate after the expiration of the 14 day period. The non-delaying party must terminate the contract

➤ Repairs – note that the Seller is not obligated to make repairs. It is paramount that the Buyer completes all Due Diligence investigations and Repair Negotiations during the DDP to avoid the loss of the EMD. A broker will prepare the Due Diligence Request and Agreement when a buyer wants to request repairs. The seller is not obligated to make repairs that are requested only those items that have been agreed to. If the seller refuses to negotiate repair, the buyer may terminate the contract – however will lose the DDF and if the DDP has expired will lose the EMD as well for breach of contract.

➤ Signatures and Dates – 1 to buy; 2 to sell (or more depending on the number of owners). The contract must be signed by both the buyer and seller the date of acceptance clearly shown. It important to remember to initial and date all changes in order to prove the date that the contract was formed.

o Other Important Topics:
➤ A broker must submit all offers immediately (but no later than 5 days) from receipt and has authority to reject an offer (even if the Seller has instructed the broker to reject offers below certain price – as this would be a violation of NCREC License Law and Commission Rules).
➤ The broker <u>cannot disclose the price or other material terms of a buyer's offer</u> to another buyer without the express permission of the buyer that made the offer.
➤ If a broker receives multiple offers they should never instruct the Seller to counter all of them at the same time as this could create the possibility of multiple contracts and potential legal disputes. A broker has to present all offers and then the Seller can decide to accept, reject or counter one of the offers, or could request that buyers bring their "highest and best" offer.

- A legally binding contract is formed when there is an offer, unconditional acceptance and communication over the wall to the offering party. It is common to see multiple questions regarding contract formation.
- The seller of a property may be an individual, multiple co-owners, or some other legal entity (partnership, LLC, Corporation). Note that a corporation is a separate legal entity where the owners hold a share of stock. Typically an individual within the organization is granted approval to purchase or sell property and therefore each shareholder would not be required to sign the contract.
- Any change to the offer (price, closing date, due diligence amount or period) is deemed a counteroffer and as such must be initialed and dated by both buyer and seller, and notice of acceptance communicated.
- Counteroffer (may become binding) vs. Memo to Buyer (not binding unless the Seller accepts the new offer)
- A seller should not knowingly transfer the property of a renter/lessee in a sales contact as this would be fraud.
- If a property is already under contract, a buyer may submit an offer with the <u>Back-Up Contract Addendum</u>. The Back-Up Contract only becomes binding when the primary contract fails. The Seller cannot accept the Back-Up and then terminate the primary contract without being in breach.
- What happens if the property is subject to lease? The lease will typically transfer with the house unless it is an estate at will, where either party may terminate without notice.
- A broker can **NEVER** <u>reference commission or disclaim liability</u> in an OPC.
- Contingencies mean that some event or item must occur in order for the contract to be binding. A contract may contain a short sale addendum – requiring the bank to approve the sales contract – which is a contingency. The seller is not obligated to sell nor the buyer obligated to buy the home prior to receiving bank approval.
- The Standard OPC is not contingent upon a buyer obtaining financing or the property appraising. For the national exam, a contract can contain a financing contingency. A buyer is permitted to terminate the contract upon written notice that buyer's loan has been denied. The seller is not obligated to extend a contingency period, although an extension could be negotiated, agreed to by all parties evidenced by a written amendment to the contract.
- Should a party seek to withdraw or terminate an offer the "over the wall" rule will apply. An Offeror has the right to withdraw the offer at any time prior to receipt of notice that the Offeree has accepted. Notice of acceptance or withdrawal will be deemed received when the client or the client's agent is notified. When a buyer is not represented (agent acting as subagent to seller), notice must be provided to the customer/unrepresented buyer to be effective.

 The Mail Box Rule states that the postmark date is the effective date of a contract as long as it is addressed to the other party or their agent. Communication must make it "over the wall" in order to be effective.

o Remedies for breach or default – both parties can mutually agree to terminate a contract with or without the return of earnest money or due diligence fee. The terms of the purchase contract will outline which party is entitled to EMD and DDF. A buyer is entitled to seek <u>specific performance</u> through the courts to force the sale of the property. It is possible to sue for actual damages in other states (Sellers in NC are entitled to EMD and DDF as sole and exclusive remedy for breach buyer when the Standard Offer to Purchase and Contract is used).

Other Contracts

- o Installment Land Contract (**Contract for Deed**) – a form of Seller financing that is very favorable to a seller. It is often used when a buyer does not have an ability to obtain financing through a bank and provides the seller with tax advantages by spreading the gain over multiple years. <u>The buyer takes possession of the property upon signing the contract</u>.
  - ➤ The buyer has <u>equitable Title</u> until the debt has been paid in full and then will receive full title (Legal Title).
  - ➤ If the Buyer defaults they will lose all money paid (total loss of equity). The equitable title received in a Contract for Deed is not the same as equitable title received when financing through a mortgage / <u>Deed of Trust</u>.
  - ➤ Should be recorded to protect against transfers to 3rd parties under the Connor Act.
  - ➤ The seller is referred to as the <u>Vendor</u> and the buyer the <u>Vendee</u>.
  - ➤ **The same rules regarding termination of a contract apply to contract for deeds as they would to any other contract to purchase real estate. The contract does not terminate if a party goes insane or dies after entering into the contract (as they were sane or alive at the time they entered into the contract). The owner would be required to honor the agreement if the vendee dies and the property passes to his/her heirs. In the event the heir defaults on the agreement, the vendor may exercise their rights and take the property back. Neither party would be required renegotiate the terms of the agreement when the property is inherited.**
- o Option to Purchase – An agreement which gives a person or entity the right to buy a property for specified period of time, typically for compensation that may or may not be applied to the purchase price.
  - ➤ <u>All of the terms of purchase are agreed to</u> up front. The period of time that a party has to exercise an option is "time is of the essence".
  - ➤ There is no standard form for this and therefore it must be prepared by an Attorney.
  - ➤ For national purposes the contract is considered unilateral until the buyer chooses to exercise the option and then the contract becomes bilateral.
  - ➤ The seller has no recourse if the buyer elects not to exercise the option to purchase the property.
- o Right of First Refusal – An open ended agreement that **should we decide to sell, we will give y the opportunity to buy before we sell it to another party**. This differs from an option where the owner has promised to sell should the optionee elect to purchase.

   Will a contract terminate upon the death of a buyer or seller? What if it is just an offer to purchase?

Questions:

o When is commission paid? Can it be paid directly to a Broker? Provisional Broker?

o What are the differences between exclusive agency and exclusive right to sell?

o When working with a buyer as a sellers subagent – how is a legally binding contract formed?

o A buyer wants to see a house that is not currently listing but is being sold FSBO. What should the broker do?

o A buyer is notified by the bank that they need 10 more days in order to close and the transaction is currently scheduled to close in 3 days. Can the seller terminate the contract? Is this considered a breach of contract and if so what remedies are available?

o The seller asked the listing agent to except the hot tub from the list of fixtures, which the agent provided for in the listing agreement and MLS listing sheet. The seller received and accepted an offer that did not include the exception. What is the result?

o The listing agent receives multiple offers for the seller's property and delivers them within the prescribed time period. One offer is for full price. The seller reviews all offers and decides he no longer wants to sell the property. Under contract law, is the seller obligated to sell the property since the buyer met all terms? Has the broker earned commission?

o Jay purchases an option for 30 days to purchase Jane's property. Fifteen days into the option period, Jay has not exercised the option. What type of contract is this – unilateral or bilateral? If Jay never exercises the option, what remedies will Jane have against him?

o What options are available to a buyer upon the expiration of the due diligence period?

o What are the 2 ways a broker can counter an offer?

North Carolina License Law and Commission Rules

o It is highly recommended that you review License Law and Rule Comments published by NCREC – located in appendix A of the Modern Practices textbook or from the Commission website. This publication provides study material for 24 out of the 40 questions that will be included on the state portion of the exam.

o Composition of the Commission – 973211

  ➢ 9 members, 7 appointed by the governor, 3 – (at least) active in real estate, 2 – (at least) not directly or indirectly involved in real estate, 1 appointed by the Speaker of the House, and 1 appointed by the President Pro-Tem of the Senate.

  ➢ Serve a 3 year term. Terms are staggered. 3 terms expire every year.

o Purpose: To protect the general public in their dealings with real estate brokers. This is accomplished by:

  ➢ Licensing real estate brokers and brokerage firms (including registration of time share projects).

  ➢ Approving schools to conduct Prelicensing, Postlicensing and Continuing Education programs approved by the Commission.

  ➢ Providing information and education relating to the real estate business to licensees and the public.

  ➢ Regulating the business activities of brokers and brokerage firms including disciplinary action (Reprimand, Censure, Suspend and Revoke).

Only the Real Estate Commission can take action against your license (R.C.S.R.). A court can only recommend that a licensee lose his/her license. The Commission grants the license and the Commission can take it away.

 A licensee must respond to a complaint within <u>14 days</u>.

 The Real Estate Commission does not currently have the ability to fine licensees (although they can fine time share developers $500 per occurrence for violations of the timeshare act).

- o The Commission CANNOT:
  - ➢ Practice law
  - ➢ Declare contracts (sales, listing or leases) void
  - ➢ Regulate commission or how fees will be shared between licensees
  - ➢ Fine licensees for violations of License Law
  - ➢ Draft or prescribe real estate contract forms (they can only prescribe what needs to be in a form – rules of the road)
  - ➢ Act as a Board of Arbitration – to settle disputes between licensees
  - ➢ Order a Broker to reimburse trust funds or compensate buyers or sellers for losses (only a court can)
- o Enforcement – can be random or upon verified complaint.
- o Causes for Suspension or Revocation of License:
  - ➢ Obtaining a license under false pretenses.
  - ➢ Licensee is convicted of felony, including failure to report the conviction within 60 days
  - ➢ Violating license law or if an unlicensed employee violates license law
  - ➢ Making willful/negligent misrepresentations or omissions of material facts
  - ➢ Making false promises
  - ➢ A Provisional Broker accepting compensation from anyone other than their BIC
  - ➢ Failing to account for all funds belonging to others
  - ➢ Being untrustworthy or incompetent so as to endanger the general public
  - ➢ Paying compensation (monetary or otherwise) to an unlicensed person
  - ➢ Fraudulent, improper or dishonest dealing
  - ➢ Performing legal services for clients (No drafting – No unauthorized practice of law)
  - ➢ Commingling personal funds with trust funds
  - ➢ Failing to deliver documents timely (immediately but no later than 5 days) or retaining documents for the prescribed time (3 years from date of last activity)
  - ➢ Violating any rule or regulation published and distributed by the Commission
  - ➢ Giving a check to the Commission that is returned unpaid (insufficient funds)

- o **When do I need to be a licensed Real Estate Broker?**
  - ➢ **LLBEANS** – When someone Lists, Leases, Buys, Exchanges, Auctions, Negotiates or Sells real property **<u>for another, for compensation</u>**.

- An individual is NOT required to be licensed when they are self-dealing (FSBO / FLBO), acting under power of attorney, a lawyer acting in the regular course of his/her law practice, appraisers, mortgage brokers, trustees, executors or administrators of an estate, salaried employee of a property management broker or the mere crier of sale at an auction.
- Licensees may hire an unlicensed assistant, however they are responsible for all actions that the assistant takes. There are different tasks that may be performed. For all brokerage activities other than property management – the assistant may perform administrative activities, however cannot show property or hold an open house. An unlicensed assistant under property management may show property and fill out preprinted forms, however cannot negotiate any terms of the rental agreement.

- Requirements to obtain Provisional License:
  - Must be at least 18 years old, a US citizen or non-citizen national or a qualified alien under federal law.
  - Pass a minimum 75 hour Prelicense course approved by the NCREC or provide evidence of equivalent experience in real estate that the Commission deems equivalent.
  - Make application and pay fee, including a background check.
  - Pass the NC Licensing Examination

- License Categories:
  - Provisional Broker – a licensee that has not completed 90 hours of Postlicensing education. In order to be active must be affiliated with a brokerage under a supervising broker-in-charge.
  - Broker – a licensee that has met the experience requirement or has completed 90 hours of Postlicensing Education.
  - Broker-in-Charge (BIC) – a full Broker with at least 2 years full time experience or the equivalent over the past 5 years that has elected to become BIC and must complete a 12 hour BIC course within 120 days of election or within the preceding 3 years. The BIC is required to supervise all Provisional Brokers as well as ensure compliance with agency disclosure and advertising of all Brokers.

    How many licenses? One license – multiple "statuses". Very important to understand the roles and limitations placed on Provisional Brokers, Brokers and Brokers-in-Charge.

  - Firm License – any form of business other than a Sole Proprietorship must have a qualifying broker and a separate firm license. So a Partnership, Limited Partnership (where some partners have contributed $$, limit liability, limited say in business), S-Corp (limited liability, income flows to return) and Corporations (limited liability, possibility of double taxation), and LLC must have a Firm License. Each office location must have a Broker-in-Charge.
  - **Limited Non Resident Commercial License** – limited to Commercial transactions (sales and leasing). The broker must be licensed in good standing in another state, must affiliate with a NC brokerage and must send declaration to the Real Estate Commission.

- Current vs. Expired - $$$$
  - Current – Paid license renewal fee by June 30th – fee must be paid online (except for unusual circumstances).
  - Expired – Failed to pay license renewal fee by June 30th.
    - Expired 6 months or less – pay $55 reinstatement fee, then submit Request to Activate.
    - Expired for more than 6 months – Pay $55 reinstatement fee and submit new application (including an updated background check). Reinstatement is not guaranteed and there are often additional requirements imposed on the licensee – completion of all outstanding Postlicensing, completion of one or more Postlicensing courses if the Broker was never Provisional, or passing the licensing exam.

- Active vs. Inactive
  - Active – Current (paid $$$), affiliated with a BIC if provisional, met Postlicensing Education Requirements and Continuing Education Requirements. (4 Hour **General** (Mandatory) **Update** + 4 Hour Elective). A BIC or BIC eligible broker must take the Broker-in-Charge Update (BICUP) + 4 Hour Elective.
  - Inactive – Current (paid $$) and 1) has decided not to affiliate with a BIC, failed to complete Postlicensing Education or Continuing Education (CE). **Inactive licensees are not required to take Postlicensing or Continuing Education but must pay the $45 license renewal fee** 2) The Broker or Provisional Broker failed to complete CE by the June 10th deadline – must take current year and make up deficiency for the previous year – for a maximum 16 hours of CE. 3) The Provisional Broker failed to complete Postlicensing Education –must complete the current year requirement and make up the deficiency.

- Proof of License – All brokerages must display a copy of the firm license at all locations. All licensees are issued a pocket card that should be carried on their person at all times while engaged in real estate brokerage activity. A copy of the pocket card must be retained by the Qualifying Broker.
- Change of Name or Address – All licensees (both Brokers and Brokerages) must notify the Commission in writing of each change of name (personal or trade) or address (personal or business) within 10 days.
- Trade Names – if a licensee is using a name other than their surname, they are required to obtain DBA (Doing Business As) assumed name certificate, file it with the County Register of Deeds and notify the Commission in writing – including a copy of the certificate.
- Delivery of Instruments – All contracts must be delivered IMMEDIATELY but no later than 5 days from the date of execution or closing with regard to the HUD-1 Settlement Statement. Property Managers are relieved of this responsibility if they provide a summary of the lease and provide a copy upon request.
- Retention of Records – 3 years from date of last activity (although recommended that you keep them longer and if you asked an attorney...forever). This includes the Working with Real Estate Agents brochure panel, listing agreements, buyer agency agreements, all versions of a contract (offer, counter-offer or offers), trust account records, and closing statements.

- Advertising Restrictions – **no blind ads** – 1) you must list that you are a licensee and the brokerage that you are affiliated with, 2) Provisional Brokers cannot advertise without the permission of their BIC and 3) must get permission from the seller to display signs on the property, use a lockbox, and advertise on the internet.
- A broker is not permitted to disclose a buyer's offer without receiving written permission from the party that made the offer (no impromptu auctions).
- An agent must disclose a bonus no later than when a prospective buyer is considering an offer. Bonuses can be money, gifts (iPad, car) or trips. In the event that an agent needs to sell multiple properties in order to receive the bonus, all buyers must be informed of the bonus. Disclosure may be made orally, however must be reduced to writing prior to writing an offer through the use of the Confirmation of Compensation form.
- Other Topics:
  - A licensee is not automatically a REALTOR®. They must be a member of Local, State and National Association of Realtors to obtain the designation.
  - A provisional broker is not permitted to perform a Broker Price Opinion (BPO) or Comparative Market Analysis (CMA) <u>for a separate fee</u>. The PB is entitled to earn a commission for the sale of the property and can prepare either a BPO or CMA for free for their client. They cannot sell the work product separately. A broker, not on provisional status, can charge a fee. The BPO cannot be used by a lender for loan origination / approval. The broker must be independent, have direct access to market information and be competent in order to prepare the BPO.
  - Can an agent purchase a client's property? This answer gets complicated as 1) the brokerage must not have a policy restricting this action 2) the seller must be informed in writing as to the risks involved and 3) the seller should be given the opportunity to seek representation from another agent within the firm or be allowed to terminate the listing.
  - Can an agent represent a buyer in the purchase of a property where the agent has an ownership interest? Generally, no. An agent selling a residential property would not be able to put the interest of their client above his/her own interest.

...ne Shares

- 5 / 5 / 5 / 10 – 5 non-consecutive periods, over 5 or more years, where the buyer has 5 days to terminate the contract and the developer must retain the purchase money in the escrow for 10 days.
- Projects must be registered with the NCREC – failure to do so while offering or selling timeshares is a <u>felony</u> offence.
- Violations of License Law by a Timeshare developer results in a fine of $500 per occurrence
- Each time share developer must disclose in a public offering statement – the total financial obligation of the purchaser including the purchase price and other charges, who can raise fees and for what reason, the date of availability of uncompleted facilities, the term of the timeshare, right to terminate within 5 days of execution, etc.
- Timeshare salesmen must be licensed and on active status to earn compensation.
- The developer is not required to be licensed, however a licensed <u>Project Broker</u> must be appointed to supervise the licensed sales staff.

NC Property Management

- NC Residential Rental Agreement Act – only applies to residential property (it's in the name). Duties cannot be waived – tenant cannot agree to live in substandard housing. (Tenant cannot abrogate rights away – as it would be contrary to public law). Rental units must be safe, fit and habitable – including smoke and carbon monoxide detectors as prescribed by law.
- In the event of breach, the landlord must use judicial means regarding eviction. The landlord cannot force the tenant out through harassment, changing locks, turning off utilities or setting belongings on the curb. Must seek legal eviction – called summary ejectment.
- Tenant cannot be evicted for requesting repairs or filing a complaint with local housing authority. Protected for up to 12 months. The landlord is not obligated to renew the lease – but must honor the initial term.
- Tenant Security Deposit Act – security deposits must be held in trust or escrow. Landlords that are not licensed brokers, that elect to hold security deposits must be bonded. A broker cannot commingle security deposits for client's rental properties with his/her own personal rental properties. Must provide an accounting of funds within 30 days, or interim accounting in 30 days and final account in 60 days.
- Maximum amount of security deposit allowed – 2 weeks if week to week; 1.5 months if month to month; and 2 months if longer.
- Foreclosure protection for tenants – if rent is at market rate and tenant is not related to the owner that is foreclosed on, then can stay for the remainder of the lease. One exception, if the new purchaser of the home will owner-occupy. In this case the tenant must be given 90 days' notice of termination. Tenant without a lease must be given 90 days' notice before termination.

Trust Funds

- Other People's Money – earnest money, security deposits, monthly rent, repair funds.
- Cannot <u>commingle</u> funds – mix other people's money with your own other than an amount to cover monthly fees and a little extra to cover fees for bounced checks (typically $100).
- Funds must be held in a bank that is federally insured and approved to do business in North Carolina (no longer required to have a physical location).
- Cash must be deposited immediately but no later than 3 days from receipt.
- EMD and Tenant Security Deposits (other than cash) must be deposited no later than 3 banking days following acceptance of the offer to purchase or lease. A licensee is permitted to safeguard the check until the agreement has been accepted.
- Rent, Settlement Proceeds and Other Trust Funds must be deposited within 3 banking days of receipt.
- Trust Account Record Keeping:
  - Must maintain complete records of all receipts and disbursements – including bank statements, cancelled checks, deposit tickets (with parties and address identified), closing statements, property management reports, contracts, leases and offers for a minimum of 3 years. A copy of all EMDs and Security Deposits checks must be retained.
  - Maintain a general ledger or check stubs identifying each transaction and showing a running balance for all funds in the trust account.

- Reconciliation of the bank statement to the ledger/journal.
- Trust account records must be made available to the NCREC for inspection upon request, without prior notice. The bank must also agree to make records available to the Commission auditor.

- Disbursement of Trust Funds - Contracts:
  - Upon withdrawal, rejection or revocation of an offer – you can return the check if you never deposited it or if deposited wait for the check to clear before disbursing.
  - Upon closing of the Transaction – Brokerage shall transfer EMD to the Operating Account if they received a net commission check (common practice in NC).
  - Upon termination of the Transaction – by mutual agreement of the parties, court order, or breach, transfer of the disputed funds to the Clerk of Court in the County in which the property is located with 90 days' notice to the parties.
- Disbursement of Trust Funds – Property Management:
  - Security deposits, rent and owner's operating expenses should flow through the trust account.
  - You cannot deficit spend – pay more expenses than you have on hand or charge anything against the security deposit prior to the tenant vacating the premises. When making repairs or paying expenses of an owner, a broker cannot spend more than the balance of funds being held for that client. For example, a broker is holding $1,000 in repair reserves and $500 for a tenant security deposit. A repair is billed for the property for an HVAC repair for $1,200. Can the broker pay the invoice form the trust account? NO! The broker would be converting other people's money. The security deposit cannot be used until the termination of the lease and only for allowable expenses. The broker can pay the bill through the operating account and bill the landlord.
  - Disburse management fees within 3o days of receipt.
  - Comply with the tenant security deposit act discussed under Property Management Section.

Real Estate Finance

- The buyer / borrower may be referred to as the mortgagor, obligor or promissor (borrower and mortgagor has oo's and rr's). Note that the buyer is giving the mortgage in return for the money.
- The lender may be referred to as the mortgagee, obligee or promise (lender and mortgagee has ee's). Note that the bank gives the money in return for the mortgage.
- A problem may refer to a borrower being required to make a 20% down payment or may state an 80% loan to value (LTV) (so 5% down payment would be 95% LTV). The amount of down payment will determine if the borrower needs to PMI (Private Mortgage Insurance) or MIP (Mortgage Insurance Premium).
- The loan to value is the lesser of the purchase price or the appraised value of the property.
- Equity is the difference between the Market Value Today less Debt Owed. Equity increases when additional payments are made to principal, capital improvements that increase the value are made, and property value appreciates.
- Interest charged on a loan is paid in arrears (July's payment pays June's interest) and is simple interest (not a compounding amount).

- Mortgage – a 2 party document between the borrower (mortgagor) and the bank (mortgagee). The borrower pledges the property as collateral to secure the loan.
- Deed of Trust – a 3 party document used to create a mortgage lien, where the borrower conveys <u>actual title</u> to a trustee that holds it for the benefit of the lender. The borrower/mortgagor/obligor will hold equitable title until the loan is paid off. Upon payoff, the defeasance clause is triggered (defeated the loan) and the trustee must reconvey the actual title to the borrower. Used in states that follow Title Theory. North Carolina is a title theory state.
- Title Theory vs. Lien Theory
  - Title Theory – the borrower retains equitable title and gives legal title to the lender which is held by a 3rd party trustee (by signing Deed of Trust = Pay to Stay). If the borrower does not pay, the trustee may foreclose on the property to satisfy the debt. It is non-judicial, faster than lien theory, and is practiced in North Carolina. It may be referred to as a foreclosure by advertisement, where the property is sold at auction.
  - Lien Theory – the borrower signs a promissory note (IOU) and retains legal title to the property. The lender must sue to obtain a judgment in order to force the sale of the property to satisfy the debt. This may be practiced in states other than North Carolina. It takes longer to foreclose on a property in a lien theory state.
- Hypothecation – pledging an asset as security for a debt, however retaining the use of the property (the opposite of layaway). A car loan is an example of hypothecation.
- Upon foreclosure, a lender may obtain a deficiency judgment (which would be a general lien against all of the borrower's assets) in the event that they do not recover enough proceeds to pay for the debt outstanding plus the costs of foreclosure.
- Common Tested Provisions – Promissory Notes:
  - Acceleration Clause – gives the lender the right to call the entire balance that is owed due and payable immediately upon default by borrower.
  - Due on Sale / Alienation Clause – the entire balance is due if the borrower transfers title without the consent of the lender.
  - Prepayment Penalty – requires the borrower to pay a penalty for paying the loan off prematurely. NC law prohibits prepayment penalties on residential loans of $150,000 or less.
  - Defeasance Clause – where the trustee must return (reconvey) the legal title to the borrower/trustee upon final payment.

  ⚠ **FHA and VA loans cannot contain prepayment penalties or due on sale/alienation clauses. These loans are assumable when a buyer qualifies. It is very important to know the difference between acceleration and alienation clauses.**

- Lending Practices and Procedures:
  - General Underwriting – the lender assesses the borrower's ability and willingness to pay debt by reviewing credit reports and scores. They determine if a borrower has sufficient assets to close the transaction, has <u>stable income</u> and adequate income to pay their obligations.
    - Evaluate housing debt as a % of gross income (debt to income ratio) – this includes principal and interest payments, property taxes, homeowner's insurance premiums, HOA fees and PMI

- Evaluation of total debt as a % of gross income – this includes housing expense and monthly recurring long term debt obligations (car loans, credit card debt, student loans, etc. with 6 months or more of payments remaining). Living expenses are not included.
- Review of credit score – FICO and information contained in a credit report.
- In addition the Underwriter will review the Property Appraisal to determine if there is sufficient collateral for the loan and if the borrower has sufficient liquid assets to close on the property.

o Types of Financing:

lein theory state

  ➢ Conventional Loans – mortgage made by a lending institution that is not insured or guaranteed by any governmental agency. Typically for 15 – 30 years where the lender sets the interest rates. Conventional lenders require 20% down payment to avoid Private Mortgage Insurance (PMI). The typical amount of gross income that can go toward housing expenses is 28% and amount of gross income that can go toward total debt is 36%
    - Total housing and other long-term debts cannot exceed 36% of gross income. Long term debts have a remaining repayment period greater than 5 months.
    - The borrower must qualify for both ratios in order to qualify for the loan.
    - Require a larger down payment and cannot carry as much debt as a borrower using FHA or VA financing.
    - If a lender wants to prevent the assumption of the loan an alienation / due on sale clause will be included in the note.
  ➢ FHA Loans - mortgage loans made by a lending institution that is insured by the Federal Housing Administration (FHA). The borrower is required to pay an up-front Mortgage Insurance Premium (MIP) for the mortgage insurance. The fee can be paid at closing or financed into the loan. FHA loans may be used to purchase 1 to 4 family homes, condominiums, townhouses and mobile homes that meet FHA minimum construction standards. The loans are only available for owner occupied properties and cannot be used by investors. FHA allows for a higher Loan-to-Value and allows for higher monthly housing and total debt ratios versus conventional loans.
    - Low down payment – as little as 3.5 %. Allows a borrower to carry more housing and long term debt.
    - 203(b) program is most often used, although FHA does have graduated and rehab loans.
    - No prepayment penalty permitted. Loans are assumable – which means the mortgage does not contain a due on sale clause.

   Interest rates are set by the bank, not FHA. Loans are made by the bank and the lender is insured by the government against losses. INSURED. INSURED. INSURED. INSURED. INSURED. FHA loans are INSURED!!!! The government insures lenders from loss due to foreclosure. This insurance, however, is <u>not</u> for 100% of the loan balance only a portion of the loan.

  ➢ VA Loans – mortgage loans made by a lending institution that are guaranteed by the VA for eligible military veterans (that have an entitlement). Loans are made to qualified veterans as well as unremarried widows or widowers. A veteran can restore their entitlement by paying the loan off in full or when an eligible veteran assumes the mortgage. VA loans <u>are assumabl</u> <u>by non-veterans</u> and all assumptions must be approved by the VA. The VA may require the veteran pay a funding fee, usually 1% of the loan amount. The fee can be financed into the loan.

- Can a non-veteran have a VA loan? Yes, if they qualify and assume the mortgage or they a a qualified unremarried widow or widower.
- Up to 100% Loan-to-Value permitted.
- No prepayment penalty permitted. Loans are assumable – which means the mortgage do not contain a due on sale clause.
- Lender sets the interest rates and terms of the loan. The government guarantees the lenc from loss due to foreclosure.

 VA loans have a higher LTV (up to 100%) and are guaranteed based on a sliding sca The Certificate of Reasonable Value (CRV) is the form completed by the VA appraise that establishes the maximum value and loan amount for a VA loan. GUARANTEED. GUARANTEED. GUARANTEED. GUARANTEED. GUARANTEED. We owe our veterans more, so loans are GUARANTEED. This guarantee is not for 100% of the loan balanc only a portion of it.

➢ Purchase Money Mortgage – seller financing is made directly from the seller to the buyer. Th may be for the first or second mortgage. The seller takes back a mortgage or deed of trust an the buyer receives the deed at closing (the owner transfers title to the buyer – note: in a title theory state with a deed of trust, the trustee will hold title).

 A seller cannot sue for a deficiency judgment in the event of a default.

➢ Rural Economic and Community Development Financing – Commonly referred to as USDA loans. The Farm Service Agency provides farmers with direct loans and loan guarantees to purchase farms. The Rural Housing Service Agency provides low to moderate income residents direct loans and loan guarantees for the purchase of 1 to 4 family homes in rural areas.

➢ Adjustable Rate Mortgage (ARM) – a loan that contains an <u>escalation clause</u> that allows the r to change at set intervals. Typically the rate is set for a certain number of years and then ma adjust every year until maturity. The beginning rate, which may be a teaser or low interest rate is also defined as the <u>start rate</u>. The interest rate may be capped as well as the amount t rate can change per adjustment period. ARMs may result in negative amortization in the eve the loan has a payment cap – as the payment would not cover the interest charged in that month.

➢ Fully amortized loan – where the buyer makes payments that include principal and interest that upon maturity of the loan, the balance will be Zero. The payments are equal throughout repayment and are larger than Term or Partially Amortized Loans since large payments are being made to the principal balance.

- ➢ Budget Mortgage – a loan where a borrower makes one payment that reflects the principal and interest payment as well as funding the escrow account for property taxes and insurance. The lender pays the property taxes and insurance when they come due.
- ➢ Partially amortized loan – will have payments to principal and interest, however the payments will not bring the balance to zero upon maturity. The borrower will either need to make a balloon payment or refinance the remaining balance. Commercial loans typically have this feature (for example a 15 year loan, with the payment determined by a 30 year amortization).
- ➢ Term / straight / interest only loan – the borrower's payment only covers the interest charge. No payment is made to principal, often for an agreed upon period of time.
- ➢ Equity is the difference between the fair market value of the property and the debt against the property (mortgage). Equity is increased when a borrower makes additional payments to the principal. Note that additional payments on a fixed loan will not change the monthly payment for the remaining term of the loan, but will decrease the number of remaining payments a borrower will need to make. In fact if a borrower made just 1 extra payment towards principal each year on a 30 year mortgage they could shave approximately 5-6 years off the loan term.
- ➢ Construction Mortgage – a short term mortgage that carries the highest risk to lenders. During the construction period the borrower typically make interest only payments and are required to take out permanent financing upon completion (**take out commitment**). The builder is able to take "**draws**" upon reaching set construction goals, not based on the money spent.
- ➢ Blanket Mortgage – used to purchase multiple parcels of land (typically for a builder) where the mortgage contains a partial release clause that allows the developer/builder to sell lots, pay off an agreed upon amount to the bank and retain some of the profit to invest in building the next home.
- ➢ Package Mortgage – mortgage for real property and certain personal property (commonly used in a resort condominium or townhouse – furnished unit).
- ➢ Reverse Annuity Mortgage – when a bank pays a property owner regular monthly payments up to a set amount or a lump sum. The bank does not receive payment until the borrower dies. Often used as supplemental income for a retiree that has substantial equity in their property. Used when a retiree does not want to sell their home, however needs to access money.
- ➢ Home Equity Line of Credit – an open ended, revolving loan that is secured by real property. The borrower can borrow up to a set limit and upon paying down the amount can borrow the money again. **This is a secured loan.**
- ➢ Home Equity Loan – similar to other mortgages, for a set amount without the revolving feature of a line of credit.
- ➢ Subprime Loan – loans to borrowers that pose increased risks based on credit scores or assets. Borrower more likely to default on the mortgage. The increased risk is reflected in the higher interest rates charged to subprime borrowers.
- o Mortgage Priority – is determined based on when the deed(s) of trust were recorded. Remember that North Carolina is a pure race state – the first to record has the higher priority. It is possible for a lender to **Subordinate** or place themselves below another lender (often occurs when a borrower refinances their first mortgage only).
- o Discount Points – prepaid interest / sunk cost. The effect of discounts points is a reduction in the interest rate on the note and a decrease in the monthly payment for the borrower. It increases the

Trade Places

yield to the lender (amount of interest earned on the note) since the borrower paid the additiona interest in advance.

> ➤ For every 1% of the loan amount the borrower receives a 1/8 % reduction in the interest rate.

> ➤ For example: If a lender is offering a loan at 6% interest with 2 discount points and a borrower has a loan of $200,000 – The borrower will pay $4,000 ($200,000 X 2%) in prepaid interest to the lender and the effective yield to the lender will be 6.25% (2/8 = .2!

o **Origination fees expressed as a percentage and discount points are both tax deductible.**

o **The <u>Federal Reserve</u> does not set interest rates on consumer loans, discount points or origination fees.**

Real Estate Finance Funding and Laws

o The Federal Reserve controls the supply of money as well as the amount of money that banks ca lend by setting reserves (the amount of money a bank cannot lend out to customers). The Fed makes loans to member banks at the discount rate which has an indirect effect of raising or lowering consumer interest rates.

o Primary Mortgage Market – Commercial banks, savings and loans, mutual savings banks, mortga companies and brokers that are lending directly to the borrower. Mortgage brokers help bring borrowers and lenders together and typically will not service the loan.

o Secondary Mortgage Market – Fannie Mae – Federal National Mortgage Association, Freddie Mac Federal Home Loan Mortgage Corporation and Ginnie Mae – Government National Mortgage Association are all major participants in the secondary mortgage market. It involves the sale of mortgage loans from direct lenders to investors – thereby making additional funds available to lend in the future.

o Fannie Mae (FNMA) purchases all types of mortgages.

Financial Legislation:

The Dodd-Frank Act, intends to prevent excessive risk taking that brought about the financial crisis in t fall of 2008. The Act created the CFPB – Consumer Financial Protection Bureau which is tasked with protecting consumers in financial transactions. One measure the CFPB has taken is the combination of RESPA and TILA into TRID – The Truth-in Lending, Real Estate Settlements Procedures Act Integrated Disclosure.

> ➤ Real Estate Settlement Procedures Act (RESPA) – **disclosure of costs to close** – applies to a federally-related <u>residential </u>mortgage loan for 1 to 4 family residences. Federally related includes VA/FHA/USDA loans, loans made by lenders whose deposits are insured by the Federal Government, or loans sold to the secondary mortgage market (so almost every loan that is not commercial or fully seller financed). RESPA identifies the costs to close (note: the brokerage commission is not included).

> • RESPA may apply based on the type of loan obtained – when a borrower obtains a residential loan that will be used to invest in commercial activity – then RESPA would

apply. When a borrower obtains a commercial loan and pledges his/her residential home as collateral – RESPA would not apply (as the borrower sought a commercial loan).

- Lender must provide a Loan Estimate (LE) within 3 days of loan application and a copy of the "Shopping for Your Home Loan" booklet. The LE details an estimate of all settlement costs. Certain costs cannot change, while some costs cannot increase in aggregate by more than 10% or lender must refund the difference and some items have no tolerance limits.
- Legal fees, title insurance and closing expenses are not considered finance charges however are required to be disclosed under RESPA.
- Must use the Closing Disclosure Settlement Statement when the borrower obtains a federally related mortgage.
- Prohibits kickbacks among service providers – referral fees (between service providers – not between brokers), gift certificates, finder fees, money, dinners, etc. for sending business between brokers, inspectors, attorneys, and lenders.

 RESPA applies to initial financing, second mortgages and Lines of Credit (which is a secured loan). RESPA does not apply to Commercial loans and 100% seller financing.

 Kids Eat Up Boogers Dirt and Lead. Kickbacks (prohibited), escrow account limits, uniform settlement statement (CD), booklet (Settlement Costs & You), disclosure of loan servicing and loan estimate within 3 days of application.

➤ Truth in Lending / Regulation Z – provides a full disclosure of the **true cost of credit.**
- Four disclosures are required if the act is triggered: The finance charge, annual percentage rate, amount financed and the total payments. Basically if you disclose 1 you must disclose them all (except annual percentage rate as this already includes the costs of borrowing).
- The law is triggered if one or more of the following are used in an advertisement: down payment, number of payments, payment amount or finance charge (interest rate). Once triggered, you are required to disclose the Annual Percentage Rate.
- General statements do not trigger Truth in Lending – low down payment, great financing available, or great rates. Note that numbers that do not relate directly to financing such as HOA dues, property taxes, broker commission, and the listing price will not trigger Regulation Z.
- Numbers that do trigger Regulation Z – 100% financing, only $500 down, payments as low as $900 per month, etc.
- Lender finance charges include origination fees, discount points, interest and assumption fees.
- Annual Percentage Rate or APR is the interest rate the borrower pays when lender finance charges are factored into the loan. The APR will be higher than the interest rate stated on the mortgage note. APR is not a trigger, however must be disclosed when a trigger term is used.
- Truth in Lending permits a borrower that is obtaining a reverse mortgage or mortgage refinance a 3 day right of rescission, where the borrower can terminate the loan.

- Equal Credit Opportunity Act – to make credit available with fairness and impartiality. Canno discriminate based on the applicant's race, color, religion, national origin, sex, marital status age. Also cannot discriminate based upon where income is derived – that any part of the applicant's income comes from public assistance (Section 8 or subsidized housing) or that a borrower has exercised his/her rights under the Consumer Credit Protection Act.
    - Lender cannot deny a loan based upon the age of the borrower – if they are qualified bank must loan.
    - Does not protect minors, sexual orientation or individuals that do not have stable income.
- Fair Credit Reporting Act – Sets standards for how credit bureaus must handle their consume credit information. It allows individuals to examine and dispute items that are on the credit report. Provides that negative information can only be reported for 7 years unless it is a bankruptcy or foreclosure which can be reported for 10 years.
- Miscellaneous Terms:
    - Usury – interest at a rate above the maximum legal rate prescribed by state law.
    - Straw Buyer – a form of loan fraud where the credit of a well-qualified borrower is substitute for a less qualified borrower.
    - Novation – used where a loan is assumed and the original borrower is no longer liable to the lender if the new borrower defaults.

Closing the Real Estate Transaction

- The buyer selects service providers – closing attorney, lender, inspector, etc. Buyer's often rely the recommendations of his/her agent.
- Settlement Meeting Method – the most common method in NC where the Attorney, the buyer and buyer's agent and the seller and seller's agent meet to transfer the property. Note that physical attendance by all parties is not required as long as all documents have been signed, notarized an funds delivered.
- The NCREC would consider a broker who fails to attend the settlement meeting with his/her clie to have violated his/her fiduciary duties to that client.
- An Agent should review the Closing Disclosure with his/her buyer or seller client to ensure that the Buyer knows the amount to bring to closing in certified funds and to determine if the seller agrees with amount of proceeds or certified check they may need to bring to closing.

     It is important to note that the Agent is <u>NOT</u> responsible for verifying EVERY amount on the closing disclosure, however is generally responsible for verifying the statements accuracy. The broker is responsible for items where they have direct knowledge. The primary source used to verify should be the Sales Contract.

- Funds and keys do not change hands until closing – the attorney performs a title search, title is updated, recorded and the lender releases funds to the attorney per the Good Funds Settlement Act.
- Escrow Settlement Method – is commonly used in many states outside of North Carolina. Usuall a third party such as a title insurance company sends a package to the buyer and seller which is signed and notarized and sent back to the title company. The title company then performs the a to close the property – title update and release of funds.

Questions:

o Which loans cannot contain an alienation or due on sale clause?

o A bank will loan based upon the lower of the _____ or _____.

o When a buyer is purchasing a vacant lot that does not have access to a public sewer system, they should perform a _____ test.

Real Estate Valuation

o **Appraisal** – is an <u>estimate of value on a given day</u> through multiple valuation methods (sales comparison, income and cost approach) which are reconciled into one. Only a licensed appraiser can perform a real estate appraisal and report on the standardized form (Uniform Residential Appraisal Report). Licensees should NEVER refer to their work as an appraisal. Appraisals are required when a borrower obtains a federally related mortgage.

o **Market Value** – An estimate of what a property may sell at assuming normal market conditions – typically motivated buyer and seller making an informed decision. **Estimate of Value.**

o **Market Price** – The actual price paid for the property when it is sold. It does not relate to cost to build. **Price Actually Paid.**

o **Cost** – the total of past expenditures, including all capital improvements made to the property and allowable closing expenses.

o **Factors that Affect Value** – physical characteristics (climate, topography, and flood zone), economic factors (employment, wages, interest rates, etc.), government regulations (zoning, building codes, etc.) and social trends (family size, population trends, etc.).

 The listing price may not be the Market Value of a property. It is often higher to allow room for negotiation. When a licensee is unsure about the probable sales price, they should list the property on the higher end to avoid "locking in" a loss.

o Commonly Tested Terms:

➤ **Supply and Demand** – Increasing supply and decreasing demand will lower prices. Decreasing supply and increasing demand will raise prices. <u>Determines the rental rates or listing price.</u> When more properties are available than buyers looking, prices will fall. When there are more buyers than available properties, prices will rise.

➤ **Substitution** – If two properties have similar utility, the one with the lower price will sell first. This is the basis for the Sales Comparison approach to value. **<u>It is considered the most important principle in appraising</u>.**

➤ **Conformity** – When homes are similar in size and architecture, the maximum value for the property will be realized.

➤ **Contribution** – The value of any part of a property is directly dependent on the degree to which it contributes to the value of the entire property. (Example: Pools are not favored in NC and in fact could negatively impact the value, however are more accepted in MA).

➤ **Anticipation** – expectation of a price change in a particular area. An investor may speculate that an area will be revitalized and therefore invest in property and potentially pay more than the current value.

- ➢ Highest and Best Use – the use that produces the maximum net return to the property owner. This can change over time as real estate markets have a life cycle.
  - o Common Approaches to Value
    - ➢ Sales Comparison Approach – the most reliable and commonly used to value residential property and vacant land.
      - • Subject Property – The property that you are valuing.
      - • Comparable or Comps – Similar recently **sold** properties (in the past 12 months), that are **sold** under typical open market conditions (properties listed on MLS, no foreclosures) with similar location, age and physical characteristics. A FSBO would not be the best comp as it has not been exposed to the competitive market.
      - • Determining the value is more art than science. Tax values do not provide the most accurate fair market value of a property as they are can be adjusted every year, however can delay adjustment to every 8 years.
      - • Brokers use recently **SOLD** comps, not ones that are active or under contract.
      - • Never adjust the Subject property
      - • If the Comp is Superior (positive features) = Subtract
      - • If the Comp is Inferior (negative features) = Increase
      - • The value for a particular item, for example a fireplace, would be determined by reviewing recent sales of comparable homes <u>both with and without the particular feature</u>. For example, Comp 1 has a fireplace and sold for $200,000. Comp 2 is very similar, except it does not have a fireplace and sold for $195,000. The value of a fireplace is $5,000.
      - • When a broker is unsure of the probable sales price, they should encourage the seller to obtain an appraisal as this is the <u>best indication of value</u>.

       The best comp is the one that SOLD with the fewest adjustments (most similar to the subject). A broker should not use active or pending homes as comps.

    - ➢ Income or Income Capitalization Approach – used for income producing properties like shopping centers, apartments, hotels, etc.
      - • Income Capitalization / Direct Capitalization: First you need to calculate the Net Operating Income
        1. **Gross Income – Vacancy and Collection = Effective Gross Income**
        2. **Effective Gross Income – Operating Expenses = Net Operating Income *Do not include depreciation, debt service or capital improvements in Operating Expenses.**
        3. **Value = NOI / Cap Rate**
        4. **Cap Rate = NOI / Value**
        5. **NOI = Value X Cap Rate**
      - **Calculating NOI is a G.I.V.E.N. = Gross Income – Vacancy – Expenses = Net Operating Income**
      - • Effective Gross Income may be referred to as **Total Anticipated Revenue**

- It is vitally important to know the formulas – as you may be asked to perform math calculations or asked about additional information that would be needed when calculating value using the income or cost approach.

 How would you calculate the CAP Rate using the income approach to value?

- Gross Rent Multiplier – a quick and dirty estimate of value for residential properties that is based on the gross income that is earned. The licensee should find recently sold properties and what their gross income was. The calculations could be <u>based upon monthly rent</u> – using the Gross Rent Multiplier (GRM) or <u>based upon yearly figures</u> using the Gross Income Multiplier (GIM). It is important that you make sure that you compare monthly rent with monthly expenses for GRM and yearly rent with yearly expenses for GIM
    1. **GRM = Sales Price / Gross Monthly Rent**
    2. **You typically perform this for 3 or more properties and then average the rate.**
    3. **Value = Gross Monthly Rent X GRM**
       OR
    1. **GIM = Sales Price / Gross Annual Rent**
    2. **You typically perform this for 3 or more properties and then average the rate.**
    3. **Value = Gross Annual Rent X GIM**

- Cost Approach – used for schools, hospitals, churches or other types of properties that are not sold often. The building value is estimated based upon the replacement or reproduction cost (NEW) less depreciation (LOSS IN VALUE). Depreciation results in a loss of utility from common wear and tear which results in a loss of value. Then an appraiser would use the sales comparison approach to calculate the value of the land and add it in to determine the property value. You do not depreciate land. The effective age of a property is more important than the actual age. Repairs / maintenance can be performed to extend the useful life of a property or impact its age. (A home built in 1920 where all major systems have been replaced and the home remodeled. The home is almost 100 years old, however would have a lower Effective Age).
- Improvements to the land may be listed in a problem. Make sure to add this to the value when determining the value of the property as a whole.
    - **Calculate the cost of the new building.**
        1. **Square Feet X Cost Per Square Foot**
    - **Calculate the depreciation.**
        2. **Cost New ÷ Useful Life X Effective Age**
    - **Calculating the value of the property.**
        3. **Cost New - Depreciation + Land + Improvements**

- Other methods for calculating depreciation – the market abstraction method – using depreciation based upon comparable properties or the breakdown method which is beyond the scope of what most brokers can perform.

- A problem may give a straight line amount of depreciation of X % per year for a certain number of years. For example 2% depreciation for 10 years – which means that the property has depreciated or lost 20% of the value.
  - o Functional Obsolescence – issue with the property itself as a result of poor design or a feature th[...] is no longer desirable (ex: 3 bedrooms 1 bath). The design is no longer desirable (having to pass through the kitchen to get to the only bathroom, or having to pass through a bedroom to get to th[...] only bathroom). It may be curable or incurable.
  - o Economic Obsolescence – caused by outside forces – outside of the property boundaries. Always incurable – zoning changes, changes to traffic patterns, more air traffic when the property is nea[...] an airport or area is becoming more industrial rather than residential.
  - o Physical Deterioration – caused by normal wear and tear – deferred maintenance. May be curab[...] or incurable.
  - o Values can be affected by economic forces (unemployment, wage levels, interest rates), by government activities (zoning, planning, building codes) or a change in the character of the area (changing from residential to commercial).

Cost   GRM

 What is the best approach for valuing a single family home? 4 unit apartment? 50 unit apartment complex? Commercial Building? Church or Post Office?

 What is the best way for a seller to determine the value of their property? Appraisal or CMA?

Landlord and Tenant

- o A lease is a contract that transfers possession of a property in exchange for rent. Two estates ex[...] – a leasehold estate for the tenant and a leased fee (freehold estate with the right of possession transferred to the tenant). The owner retains all other rights, including the right to sell the property, however the sale will be subject to the lease (new owner must honor the lease terms). Which party gets the fee? The owner gets the fee and therefore has a leased fee interest in the property. Which party has a hold on the property? The tenant has a hold on the property and therefore has a leasehold interest in the property.

 Leases that exceed 3 years must be in writing under the Statute of Frauds and must be recorded in order to be protected against 3rd parties under the NC Connor Act. So, an ora[...] lease may be valid between the current owner and renter, however if the property is sol[...] without the lease being recorded the lease would be unenforceable.

Types of Lease Estates:
  - ➤ Estate for Years – definite end date...does not have to be for a year just a fixed time period. Automatically terminates without notice on the end date.
  - ➤ Estate from Year-to-Year – periodic tenancy that automatically renews until the required notice is provided by either party.
  - ➤ Estate at Will – an estate where either party may terminate without notice.

- ➢ Estate at Sufferance – where a tenant has refused to vacate a property (holdover tenant) and no longer has legal right of possession. The owner must seek eviction through judicial means.
- o Types of Leases:
  - ➢ Fixed or Gross - The tenant pays a set rental amount and the landlord pays all costs of ownership (maintenance, property taxes and insurance).
  - ➢ Net – The tenant pays a base rent as well as some or all of the costs of ownership (maintenance, property taxes and insurance). You may hear of a Triple Net Lease – this is where the tenant pays all costs of ownership without taking title to the property.
  - ➢ Percentage – Commonly used in retail leases where the tenant pays a base rent plus a percentage of sales/income.
  - ➢ Graduated – Rent increases or decreases at set intervals
  - ➢ Index – Rent increases or decreases based upon some widely used economic indicator (consumer price index, etc.)
  - ➢ Ground – Land lease where the term is typically for an extended period of time (often 99 years with the option to extend for another 99 years) where the tenant pays for the construction of a building and other owner expenses. The ownership of the land is separate from the ownership of the building.
  - ➢ Full Service – Included in the tenant's rent is the space plus security, janitorial services, utilities and maintenance.
- o Compensation – the management fee is negotiable between the owner and the broker/brokerage. There is no "usual or customary" fee as that would be a violation of the Sherman Antitrust Act.
- o North Carolina Residential Rental Agreement Act – The landlord must provide safe, fit and habitable premises to a tenant that is renting a residential dwelling. This includes complying with building codes, maintenance and repair of appliances, electrical, plumbing and HVAC systems among others. Changing HVAC filters or replacing the wax seal on the toilet is a preventative repair. Patching the roof would be an example of an ongoing repair. For National purposes – may reference the Uniform Residential Landlord Tenant Act.
- o The tenant cannot make an agreement to rent a property that is not safe, fit and habitable (**abrogation**) so the landlord would have to make repairs. Tenants cannot sign away certain protections that are provided for under state/federal statutes.
  - ➢ Landlord must provide working smoke detectors. In addition carbon monoxide detectors must be installed on each level of the rental unit that has an attached garage or fossil fuel burning appliance / fireplace (and replace batteries at the beginning of the tenancy).
  - ➢ The Tenant must keep the premises clean and remove his/her trash, maintain the plumbing fixtures (not repair if leaking), and not damage the property (except for normal wear and tear). Tenants must replace the batteries in the smoke and carbon monoxide detector during the tenancy.
  - ➢ No Retaliatory Eviction – the landlord cannot seek eviction of a tenant if they exert their right to safe, fit and habitable premises and request repairs through court action or filing a complaint with the local housing authority. This protection is for up to 12 months.
- o North Carolina Tenant Security Deposit Act – law that limits the amount that can be charged based on the length of the lease agreement, the types of charges that are allowable against the deposit, and where the security deposit must be held.

- The maximum-security deposit is 2 weeks for week to week, 1.5 months from month-to-mon and 2 months for lease terms greater than one month.
- Reasonable pet deposits are allowed, however cannot be charged for service dogs.
- The landlord or property manager can charge back rent, late fees, damages to the premises (above normal wear and tear), period of time the unit is not rented during the lease rental period, court costs/legal fees, and the costs of re-renting the premises against the security deposit. Large holes in a wall would be above normal wear and tear. Worn carpet in a high traffic areas would not.
- A detailed accounting of the charges must be provided within 30 days of the termination of the tenancy. If the final costs have not been tallied an interim accounting must be provided in 30 days and a final accounting must be provided within 60 days of termination.
- The security deposit must be held in a trust or escrow account if handled by a licensee or a non-licensee may elect to be bonded. If the security deposit is not handled in this manner the landlord/property manager loses the right to charge any of the costs outlined above against the security deposit.

Property Management

- A Property Manager that is earning commission or fees on behalf of another is required to be licensed under North Carolina License Law.
- An agent typically acts as a General Agent – where they can bind the landlord to lease agreement but cannot sell the property, make capital improvements or reinvest the profits.
- When representing a tenant, an agent will act as a special agent. Tenant representation is not common in North Carolina.
- Note that there are exemptions to the licensing requirement:
  - W-2 Employee or officer of a corporation for the benefit of the entity (FSBO / FLBO) – dealing with transactions that are for the benefit of the company and not a 3rd party.
  - An unlicensed assistant that is working for a licensed broker – can show property, fill in pre-printed lease forms however cannot negotiate lease agreements.
- Property Managers are typically compensated based on rent collected. They may also receive a minimum fee for when the unit is unoccupied or the tenant is not paying. The compensation is negotiable between the brokerage and client.
- Property Managers Duties – 1) Establish a rental schedule – where the most important factor is the rent charged by comparable properties; 2) Preparing an operating budget – for the calendar year and sometimes for 3-5 years in advance; 3) Market and rent the property – while complying with Fair Housing (see below); 4) Collecting rent and security deposits – and accounting for them according to the NCREC License Law and Commission Rules; 5) Maintaining and protecting the property; 6) Taking legal action – to evict tenant or recover rent; and 7) Reporting – providing monthly accounting of income/expense, summary of lease agreements entered into on behalf of the client and providing copies of lease agreement when requested.
- The best way to avoid issues with tenants is to properly screen them before agreeing to rent and to use the Commission's Renting Residential Real Estate Pamphlet as it covers the duties of both landlords and tenants.

- A property manager can hire unlicensed assistants to help them in performing his/her property management duties. Unlike other forms of brokerage, the unlicensed assistant performing property management duties can show property, fill out pre-printed lease forms, however cannot negotiate lease terms (decrease in rent, rental term, security deposit).
- Property managers typically cannot pay the owner's income taxes, reinvest profits on behalf of the owner, or determine capital improvements.
- When an owner hires a property manager they lose any right that they may have to discriminate against a tenant based on State / Federal protected classes. (See Fair Housing Below)
- An agent has a duty to inform the owner about adverse conditions or decisions that an owner may make that would negatively impact the ability to rent the home. The owner has the ultimate decision on how to proceed. If an owner is doing something that violates the law, the agent should ask the owner to remedy the situation. Should they fail, the broker should terminate the property management agreement.
- Federal Protection for Tenants at Foreclosure – applies to any federally related mortgage on a residential dwelling that is rented. The tenant must have a lease that is near market rent and cannot be a relative of the owner. If the lease is oral or if the buyer will owner occupy the foreclosed residence – buyer may give 90 days' notice to vacate.
- North Carolina Foreclosure Protection – A tenant can terminate the lease agreement without penalty with 10 days' notice to the landlord if the tenant receives notice that foreclosure is imminent and there are fewer than 15 rental units.
- Cash flow is determined by taking into account all the money that comes in (rent, additional income) less going out for expenses (bad debts, vacancy, operating expenses and debt service). When money is left over after paying expenses the property has a positive cash flow.
- Types of Eviction:
  - Summary Ejectment – where the landlord seeks actual eviction of the tenant as a result of the tenant breach of the lease (often for the failure to pay rent). The owner can sue for failure to pay however all action will stop if the tenant pays the back rent amount plus late/court fees. The owner can also sue for the actual breach of the agreement event if the tenant remedies the breach (making payment). The landlord must use JUDICIAL means and cannot "Self Help" by turning off utilities or removing belongings.
  - Constructive Eviction – when the owner fails to maintain safe, fit and habitable premises. For example if the HVAC system fails and the owner has not taken steps to correct the matter even though the tenant provided written notice, the tenant can elect to move out without penalty and sue the landlord for the cost of the move, temporary housing, and recovery of rent paid while the unit was not habitable. The tenant can elect to stay (however must still pay unless court orders otherwise), can seek action through the court or by reporting the violation to the Housing Department.

North Carolina Vacation Rental Act

- "Recreational Rentals" for lease terms of 90 days or less.
- Same requirements of the landlord – safe, fit and habitable and the tenant – pay and not damage.
- If a property is sold the new owner must honor lease agreement that terminate within 180 days from the date of sale.

- o Security deposits must be held in a trust or escrow account – no ability to be bonded, however the owner may spend up to 50% of the security deposit prior to the rental period.
- o Provides for accelerated eviction.
- o Permits the payment of a referral fee to unlicensed travel agents under certain circumstances.

Federal and State Fair Housing

- ➢ It is important to apply the facts of a question and answer based upon the information provided and the law being tested.
- ➢ Federal Civil Rights Act of 1866 – Contains the blanket statement that "All citizens of the US shall have the same right in every state and territory as enjoyed by white citizens thereof to inherit, purchase, lease, sell, hold and convey real and personal property." Prohibits discrimination based upon **RACE, ancestral and ethnic characteristics,** when selling or renting real or personal property. There are no exceptions to this law. Enforced by private lawsuit only.
- ➢ Federal Fair Housing
- o Housing and Urban Development (HUD) was **established in 1965**. They hear complaints regarding the Federal Fair Housing Act of 1968.
- o Federal Fair Housing Act of 1968 – Applies to residential real estate and prohibits discrimination when selling or renting real property.
- o Fines of $16,000 for first offense / $65,000 for subsequent offenses. Fines can be increased to $100,000 per offense if the Justice Department becomes involved – based upon a pattern of discrimination.
- o The best protection for a broker is to keep complete and accurate records of the transaction.
- o Protected Classes:

F – Familial Status	**C** – Color
R – Race	**O – OPPORTUNITY**
E – EQUAL	**R** – Religion
S – Sex	**N – National Origin**
H – Handicap	

 Handicap – landlord must allow tenant to make changes (for a ramp, widen doors, etc.) at the tenant's expense. A tenant "**MAY**" be required to return the unit to its original state prior to changes. A tenant "may" be required to provide the owner with additional funds to cover the cost of major modifications.

 Familial Status – families with children under 18 years of age, including pregnant women. Can be discriminated against if it is a retirement community (55 and older). A landlord can refuse to rent to a family when the size exceeds local occupancy limit for the unit.

 Sexual Orientation, Marital Status, Undergraduate Students are not a protected classes. If an owner did not want to rent to female undergraduate students, then they would violate fair housing as they are discriminating on the basis of sex.

Exemptions to Federal Fair Housing Law:

- Apply to owner(s) that sell property without the assistance of a licensee as long as they do not own more than 3 residential homes and do not use discriminatory advertising.

 **Note that this exemption applies to Federal Fair Housing and not the Federal Civil Rights Act of 1866.**

- Rental of a 1-4 unit residential dwelling as long as one of the units is owner occupied.
- **Religious organization** renting or selling units for the benefit of their members rather than for profit.
- Private club as long as they are not discriminating based upon race.
- There are certain restrictions for Senior Only Housing (55 and older communities). Note that if a person is over 55 and wants an agent to steer them away from neighborhoods with children and the agent complies, this would violate fair housing regulations. A senior could state that they want to live in an approved 55 and older community which is not considered steering.

  Note: Sex was added in 1974 and Familial Status and Handicap were added in 1988. The law prohibits:

- <u>Blockbusting</u> – Encouraging or inducing the sale of property by creating panic that a particular race is moving into the neighborhood.
- <u>Steering</u> – Directing or channeling. Trying to get a buyer to purchase a property in a particular neighborhood based on the protected classes.
- <u>Redlining</u> – Lender refusing to lend to a particular geographic area that is not based on buyer's qualifications.
- Discriminatory Advertising – stating that a certain protected class is not welcome or by depicting only one race, gender or ethnicity.
- Lying about the status of a property – that is has been rented or sold when in fact it has not.

o Enforced by filing a complaint with HUD that may be referred to the NC Human Relations Commission.

o HUD must make a determination within **100 days** <u>of receiving the complaint</u>.

o The party filing the complaint with HUD <u>must file within **1 year**</u> of the potential discrimination (aggrieved party has 2 years to file a civil complaint directly in federal court).

o A broker should advertise information about the property not about the people that should or should not live there.

o Upon complaint – HUD will consider results of testing studies performed on the company, the properties that were shown to the buyer or tenant by the broker, and if the equal opportunity poster is displayed in the office.

o HUD will not consider the brokers intent – you can be in violation based upon the appearance of your actions.

o What classes are not protected? – Age, sexual orientation, gender identity, marital status or occupation. Keep in mind that REALTORS cannot discriminate on any basis – cannot violate State / Federal Fair Housing, 1866, and cannot violate association rules.

- State Fair Housing Act – is identical to the Federal Fair Housing Act as amended except for the exemptions:
  - No exemption for sale of property even if the owner is selling FSBO, based upon race. The owner cannot discriminate under the act.
  - Owner can discriminate for 1-4 unit rental if owner occupied or if 1 of the occupants is a relative.
  - Single Sex Dormitory – allowed under the act.
  - Enforced by filing a complaint with the North Carolina Human Relations Commission

- Americans with Disabilities Act (ADA) – requires businesses (commercial facilities, banks, hotels, etc) to be accessible to persons with physical or mental disabilities. Businesses can be fined for failure to comply with the act or may not be able to operate (injunction) until they comply. An owner of an apartment complex must have handicap accessible units for all buildings built after 1992. An owner is required to make reasonable accommodations.
  - The owner of a rental property must allow a tenant to make alterations to a property at the tenant's expense.
  - Some alterations do not need to be returned to the original state after the end of the tenancy – such as widened doorways, pull bars or wheelchair ramps (so the tenant "MAY" be required to return the property to its original state).
  - Some modifications would cost a significant amount of money to return the property back to its original state – such as lower cabinets – and therefore the owner can charge a reasonable amount of funds and retain them in an escrow account.

Questions:
  - Can an owner discriminate based upon a tenant's criminal history (drug dealing, violent history)
  - Can an owner choose not to rent to a prospective tenant that is addicted to drugs, however is seeking treatment?
  - Can a landlord refuse to rent to an individual that has recovered from a mental issue?
  - In what manner can a landlord refuse to rent to family with children?
  - Would a seller be liable for brokerage commission if they refuse to rent/sell property based upon a protected class?
  - How many units can a property have and still qualify for an exemption under federal fair housing
  - Would a landlord with a no pet policy need to rent to a tenant that has a comfort animal such as dog, bird, or snake?
  - Would a landlord be required to make an accommodation for a tenant that develops a handicap during tenancy? What if the handicap is for someone that moves in with the tenant (assuming it does not violate local occupancy regulations?

Basic Real Estate Investment

  - Equity – the difference between what the property is worth and what is owed. It increases when payments are made on an amortized loan, additional payments made to principal, when capital improvements are made or when values appreciate.

- Appreciation – the increase in value over time (keeping in mind that property values can decrease as well).
- Leverage – Use of Other People's Money – Using borrowed money to finance an investment. It increases the risk but also the return on investment to the investor.
- Cash Flow After Debt Service or Before Tax Cash Flow:
  Recall G.I.V.E.N. for calculating NOI. Gross Income – Vacancy – Expenses = NOI
  NOI – Debt Service = Before Tax Cash Flow
- Cash on Cash Rate of Return = Before Tax Cash Flow / Down Payment
- For National Exam –may be asked about After Tax Cash Flow. When that occurs you would perform the above calculation, then you would subtract out income taxes.
- Return on Investment (National):
  Before Tax Cash Flow – Income Tax = After Tax Cash Flow
  After Tax Cash Flow / Equity

Federal Income Taxation of Real Estate

- It is common to be tested on what expenses may be deducted on the current years federal income tax return and what the gain is for a particular property.
  - Tax Deduction = Property Taxes, Interest and Points (paid for purchase not refinance) and origination fees expressed as a percentage
  - Calculation of gain is done in three steps:
    1. **Calculate Adjusted Basis = Purchase Price + Allowable Closing Costs (not finance charges) + Capital Improvements**
    2. **Calculate Amount Realized = Sales Price – Commission – Allowable Closing Costs (not repairs)**
    3. **Calculate Gain = Amount Realized – Adjusted Basis**
- Taxation on the gain from the sale of a principal residence receives special tax treatments – as long as it is your primary residence for 2 out of the last 5 years – you can exclude $250,000 of gain if single / $500,000 of gain if married. Cannot be used more than once every 2 years.
- Capital Gains Rates – 12 months or less – short term gain taxed at ordinary rates / More than 12 months – reduced tax rate
- Federal Taxation of Real Estate Investments – Owner can deduct mortgage interest, real property taxes, repairs & maintenance, insurance, utilities, supplies, advertising, management fees, salaries, depreciation and Mandatory HOA dues.
- **1031 Like-Kind Exchange** – Investment for Investment – never for your personal home. As long as you reinvest your boot (amount realized) you will not have to pay taxes. The basis you have in the current investment transfers over to the new property or properties that you purchase. It is recommended that a licensee refer his/her client to a qualified attorney to handle the exchange. There are too many rules to follow, where any violation could result in the transaction being fully taxable. The client will have 45 days from the date of sale of his/her property to identify potential replacements. The client will only be able to purchase property that is included on the list. The client must close on the property/properties within 180 days from the sale of the old property.

- When property is inherited – the basis is increased to the market value at the time of death. When the property is sold gain or loss will be determined based upon this stepped up basis rather than the tax basis of the deceased.
- The amount owed on a mortgage has no bearing on taxable gain or loss – the seller may have to pay capital gain taxes on the sale of a property where they did not receive money, in fact may have been required to pay money in order to close and release liens.

Environmental Hazards

➢ A broker that is aware of environmental contamination to groundwater, leaking storage tanks or other hazard, must disclose to buyers as this is a material fact. A broker that is aware of contamination of neighboring properties should also disclose this fact to potential buyers, even if the seller believes that the contamination has been contained, cured or remediated.

➢ When a buyer is interested in purchasing property that has been used for commercial or industrial activities, such as a car dealership, gas station, chemical manufacturer, dry cleaner, etc., the broker should recommend environmental testing be performed.

➢ While the EPA enacts legislation and can provide information about the dangers regarding environmental contamination, they are not the primary resource a buyer would use or an agent would recommend when a buyer is evaluating a property for purchase.

➢ The broker should refer the buyer to an Environmental Specialist that can perform tests and evaluate the existence or level of contamination on a site. When purchasing commercial property a lender may require phase I environmental testing.

➢ The broker should not rely upon his/her own investigation of the property, a call to the EPA, or consultation with an attorney. The property should be evaluated by an Environmental Engineer.

➢ **CERCLA / Superfund** – the Comprehensive Environmental Response, Compensation, and Liability Act – established a fund to clean up hazardous waste and created a process for identifying potentially responsible parties (note the current owner bears the greater share of the cost even if they did not the cause of the contamination). Properties that contain high levels of contamination may qualify as a Superfund site.

➢ Lead Based Paint – causes serious damage to the brain, kidneys and nervous system. It accumulates in the body and cannot be processed out. Causes developmental delays and possible retardation. Increase risk for homes that are built prior to 1978.
- Under the **1992 Residential Lead Based Paint Reduction Act** a seller must disclose if they know of the presence of lead in the home or have reports about lead based paint in the home. Agents must ensure that the disclosure form is completed and that the pamphlet "Protecting Your Family from Lead in Your Home" is provided. This applies to properties listed with a broker or offered FSBO or FLBO.
- The buyer is permitted to inspect the property for the presence of lead – nationally they have 1 days; in NC they should inspect during the due diligence period.
- Tenant should be provided with lead based paint disclosure as well as pamphlet. The landlord does not have to grant a tenant an opportunity to test for the presence of lead or force the landlord to have it removed.

- The seller/landlord is not required to obtain a lead based paint inspection, nor are they required to pay for its removal.
- Encapsulation is the most common method used to protect against the hazards of lead paint.
- Lead is often found in paint, dust, in soil and on pipes, however rarely found in wall insulation.
- Remediation may be required when more than a 6' x 6' area is disturbed or when windows are replaced.

 The seller does not have to certify that a home is lead free and is not required to remediate. A buyer that elects to inspect the property must pay for the inspection, unless otherwise provided for in the contract.

- Radon – a colorless, odorless and tasteless radioactive gas that naturally dissipates in the air however may become trapped in houses. In concentrations greater than **4.0 picocuries** (according to EPA) lung cancer can result. Installation of a ventilation system or exhaust fan can dissipate the gas. Radon is not tested by using polybutylene piping (plastic pipe that may leak).
- Asbestos – commonly used for insulation and as siding prior to its ban in 1978. When it becomes friable – decays and becomes airborne – it can cause cancer (mesothelioma) and respiratory diseases. Risk is reduced through encapsulation or remediation.
- Mold – not all mold is hazardous - it must be tested prior to representation that it is a health risk. Mold requires moisture to grow so can be mitigated by reducing or eliminating moisture sources (french drains, pumps, fans, dehumidifiers). When present in walls, it may be considered toxic and require remediation. Nationally, the seller must disclose mold presence in a house. A broker is responsible for disclosing what they know or reasonably should have known (if they notice a musty smell, high humidity or evidence of water damage).
- Carbon monoxide – gas created from combustion – natural gas, liquid petroleum, wood, gas, etc. Home should be property ventilated to avoid risk of death.
- Urea-formaldehyde - found in insulation and treated lumber.
- Methamphetamine Labs – material fact as the house will be contaminated and depending upon disposal of chemicals the grounds and groundwater may be contaminated.
- Contaminated groundwater and leaking underground storage tanks – material fact when it occurs on the property or has occurred on neighboring property.
- North Carolina Environmental Laws:
    - NC Leaking Petroleum Underground Storage Tank Cleanup Act – regulates the discharge of oil or other hazardous chemicals. Homeowners may bear the cleanup expenses even if they did not install, fill or use the oil.
    - NC Sediment Pollution Control Act – The act calls for erosion control, buffer zones and sedimentation plans in any type of development, construction or other activity that may disturb vegetation.
    - NC Dredge and Fill Act – requires a permit prior to dredging or filling waterways.
    - NC Coastal Management Act – controls development to land located in coastal areas and is designed to protect and preserve wetlands.
    - NC Mountain Ridge Protection Act – allows municipalities to adopt and enforce ordinances that regulate the construction of tall buildings.

Residential Construction

- o Building Codes – minimum construction standards for new construction, renovations or additions. It is very important to follow permitting requirements. This is an area of significant focus in practice and is the "new mold".
- o General Contractors License – required when an individual or entity is building a structure costing more than $30,000.
- o Properties that have an air handler and ductwork have a <u>forced air</u> HVAC system.

Basic Terminology:

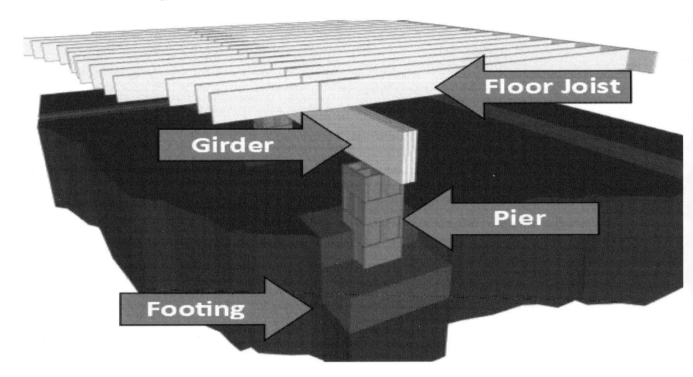

- ➢ Footing – A concrete support that forms the base of the foundation that is poured below the frost line under the surface of the ground and used to distribute weight evenly. Hint: What is the base of your foundation – your **foot**'ing!!
- ➢ Piers – a foundation column that supports the floor framing over an open span between the foundation walls.
- ➢ Girder – Heavy wooden member or steel beam that typically runs across the top of the piers and supports the floor joists. Hint: Think Girdle – holds in the center…and a girder holds up the center.
- ➢ Joists – part of the floor framing - attached to the sill.

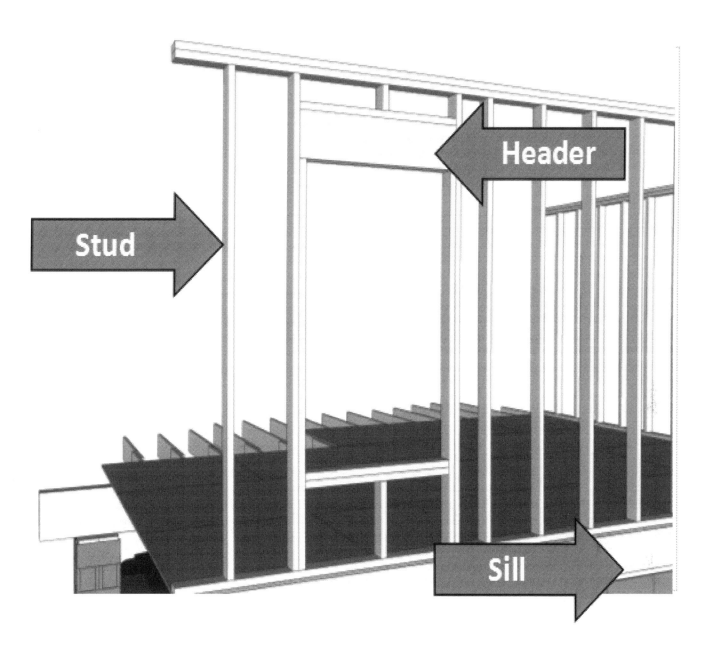

Wall Components:

- ➤ Studs – Part of the wall framing, commonly 2" x 4" wood that is attached to the sill plate.
- ➤ Header – Support beam located above openings – typically doors and windows – meant to strengthen the wall by spreading the weight.
- ➤ Sill or Sill Plate – lowest wooden member in home construction that rests upon the foundation wall and top of the piers.

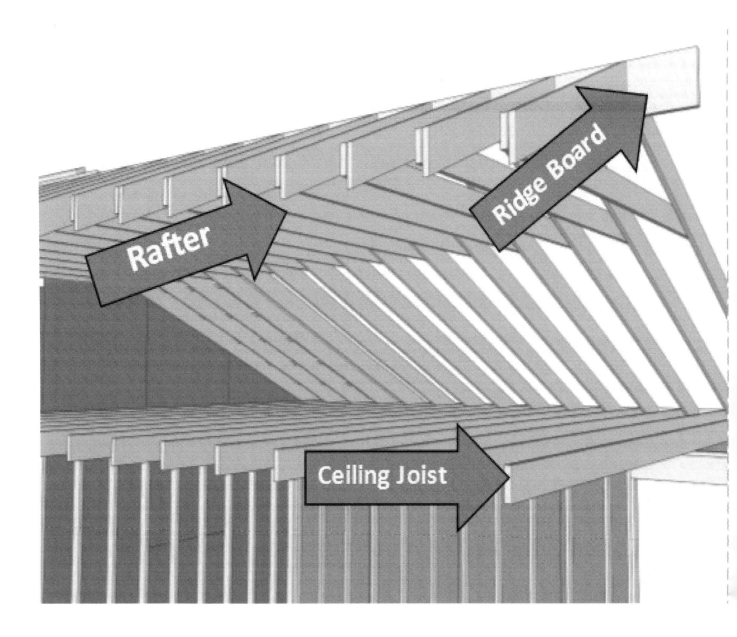

o Roof Components:

➤ Sheathing – the wooden layer attached to the roof rafters (and wall studs); most often plywoo
or OSB.
➤ Roof Pitch – the slope of a roof is calculated as the rise over run.
➤ Ridge Board – often tested as the highest wooden member in roof construction that is fastened
to the ends of the rafters.
➤ Rafter – a type of beam that supports the roof that extends from the ridge to the wall plate.
➤ Flashing – sheet metal that protects the building from water damage – found around chimney

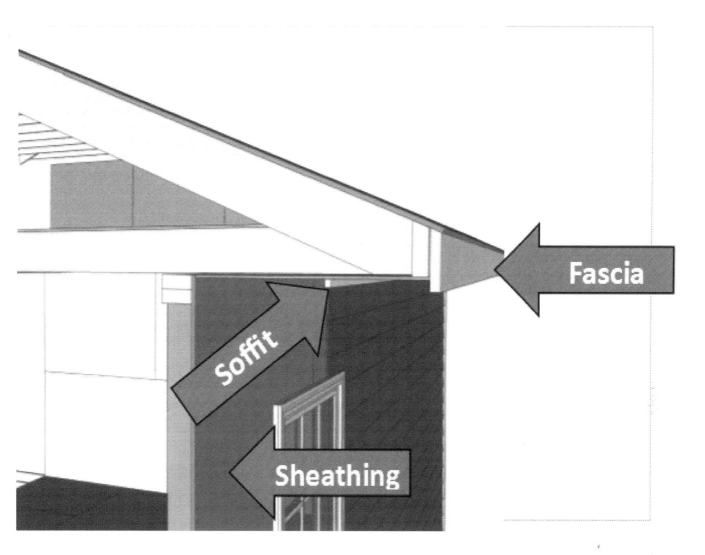

- o Eave – the overhang of the roof over the wall stud.
  - ➢ Fascia – component of the eave that faces out and where the gutter is typically attached to.
  - ➢ Soffit – the flat board attached to the eave.

Other Terms:
- o Windows – contain muntins – horizontal bars separating glass panes, mullions – vertical bars separating glass panes and sashes – framed part of window that holds glass in place.
- o Septic System – require percolation test (**perc or perk**) to determine the suitability of the soil and which system will work, if any, to ensure proper leaching takes place. Soil suitability permits are issued by the local health department and detail a specific number of bedrooms the dwelling can have.

Answers to Questions Previously asked in Workbook

Pg. 5.

- When a seller fails to exclude a fixture from the Offer to Purchase and Contract such as a family heirloom, are they required to transfer it or can they replace the item with a similar quality fixture? **The seller will be required to transfer the fixture.**
- A tenant is renting commercial space for a restaurant where trade fixtures have been installed. Upon termination of the lease can the tenant remove the trade fixtures? **Tenant must remove trade fixtures prior to termination.** What if the trade fixtures are abandoned? **They become the real property of the landlord.**
- What is the term that defines the sudden loss of land that would not result in a change in the property line? **Avulsion.**

Pg. 8.

- Which forms of ownership contain the right of survivorship? **National Joint Tenancy and Tenancy by the Entirety.** What does right of survivorship mean? **Upon death of tenant, their share of the property transfers to the other tenant(s), not their heirs.**
- A married couple owns property under Tenancy by the Entirety, and has separated. What impact will this have on the current form of ownership? **None.**
- The owner of a condo defaults on his mortgage. What can the bank legally seek as a remedy? **Foreclosure of the individual unit, not the entire condominium.**
- Who owns the common elements in a townhome community? **HOA.**

Pg. 9.

- Is an owner protected from an adverse possession claim if they suffer from a handicap, making it difficult to detect? **No.**
- What is the difference between a lien and an encumbrance? **A lien is a financial type of encumbrance. Encumbrances are any easement, restriction, liens or other claim against the property that could diminish the value of the property.**
- Which form of co-ownership cannot be subject to a suit for partition? **Tenancy by the Entirety.**
- What law prevents a creditor from enforcing a lien against a property? **Homestead Exemption.**
- _____ prevents a neighbor from causing damage to your property when excavating or mining their property? **Right to Subjacent/Lateral Support.**

Pg. 12-13

- Can an owner of a property prevent condemnation? **No.**
- What happens when a property is taken through eminent domain when the property is subject to a lease agreement? **Lease agreement is terminated.**

- A property owner would not have to go through the formal rezoning process if they qualify for a _____? **Special Use Permit.**
- Verizon files for bankruptcy protection. What happens to the easements that they own? **They can be transferred. (Commercial Easement in Gross).**
- Tony purchases a property that has an appurtenant easement to cross a neighbor's property. He has not visited his property for 5 years, thus has not used the easement. Can the owner of the servient deem the easement abandoned? **No. Non-use alone does not constitute abandonment. The owner must pursue removal of the easement and recordation.**

Pg. 18

- How can a deed be valid but unenforceable? **If it has not been recorded.**
- What is the covenant of seisin? **Indicates seller has ownership and right to convey the property.**
- What is a habendum clause? **Defines or limits the extent of ownership.**
- _____ protects an owner against claims that are not a matter of public record? **Extended Title Insurance Policy.**
- What is indemnity? **An agreement to compensate for a loss.**

Pg. 20

- What happens if the broker leaves? **The general agency agreement between the agent and firm is terminated.** Can the broker take the listing? **It depends on what the agreement between the broker and the firm states regarding termination and who retains the clients.**

Pg. 22

- Which type of agency affords a client with greater representation – dual or designated? **Designated, which is a form of dual agency.**

Pg. 23

- A Seller tells the listing agent that there is a foundation issue but instructs the agent not to disclose. If the agent complies what are they guilty of, if anything? **Willful Omission.**
- What would an agent be guilty of if they fail to disclose the existence of restrictive/protective covenants, since the subdivision was located outside of their normal selling area and they were therefore unaware? **Negligent Omission.**

Pg. 29

- When would a seller not be liable to pay a commission to a broker upon the sale of his/her property to a buyer? **In an open listing or exclusive agency agreement, where the seller procured their own buyer.**

- What are the differences between execute, executory, and executed? **Signed, Under contract preparing for closing, Closed.**
- Would a seller that discovers they have contracted with a minor be allowed to void the contract? **No, only the minor.**
- What are the essential elements of a deed? **IGPWED; In writing, Grantor competent, Property description, Words of conveyance, Execution by grantors only, Delivery and acceptance.** A contract? **Mutual Assent, Consideration, Capacity of parties, Lawful Objective.**
- Would an agent be responsible/liable for failing to disclose an issue such as standing water in the crawlspace during spring time, when the listing is taken in the fall and no evidence of past standing water is evident? **No, unless the seller mentions it, at which point it now becomes material fact that the agent is aware of and must disclose.**

Pg. 30

- What happens if the buyer signs a promissory note for the EMD? **This is a separate agreement between the buyer and seller. Lender must be provided a copy.** Is this part of the mortgage? **No.**

Pg. 32-33

- Will a contract terminate upon the death of a buyer or seller? **No. The contract is binding on heirs and assigns.**
- When is commission paid? **Typically after closing.** Can it be paid directly to a Broker? **Yes.** Provisional Broker? **No.**
- What are the differences between exclusive agency and exclusive right to sell? **EA – 1 agent; competes with seller. ERTS – seller must pay commission regardless of who is procuring cause of the sale.**
- When working with a buyer as a sellers subagent – how is a legally binding contract formed? **Buyer must be directly informed of seller's acceptance of the offer.**
- A buyer wants to see a house that is not currently listed but is being sold FSBO. What should the broker do? **Contact seller to find out if they will compensate an agent bringing a buyer, and review WWREA with them and get a compensation agreement signed prior to showing the property.**
- A buyer is notified by the bank that they need 10 more days in order to close and the transaction is currently scheduled to close in 3 days. Can the seller terminate the contract? **No.** Is this considered a breach of contract and if so what remedies are available? **No.**
- The seller asked the listing agent to except the hot tub from the list of fixtures, which the agent provided for in the listing agreement and MLS listing sheet. The seller received and accepted an offer that did not include the exception. What is the result? **Seller must leave the hot tub with the property.**
- The listing agent receives multiple offers for their seller's property and delivers them within the prescribed time period. One offer is for full price. The seller reviews all offers and decides he no

longer wants to sell the property. Under contract law, is the seller obligated to sell the property since the buyer met all terms? **No.** Has the broker earned commission? **Yes.**

o   Jay purchases an option for 30 days to purchase Jane's property. Fifteen days into the option period, Jay has not exercised the option. What type of contract is this – unilateral or bilateral? **Unilateral.** If Jay never exercises the option, what remedies will Jane have against him? **None.**

o   What options are available to a buyer upon the expiration of the due diligence period? **Complete the transaction, or terminate with loss of EM.**

o   What are the 2 ways a broker can counter an offer? **Orally or in writing.**

Pg. 47

o   Which loans cannot contain an alienation or due on sale clause? **FHA/VA and any other assumable loans.**

o   A bank will loan based upon the lower of the _____ or _____. **Contract Sales Price or the Appraised Value.**

o   When a buyer is purchasing a vacant lot that does not have access to a public sewer system should perform a ____ test. **Perk.**

Pg. 49

o   How would you calculate the CAP Rate using the income approach to value? **Use GIVEN to determine NOI, then divide it by the Market Value.**

Pg. 50

o   What is the best approach for valuing a single family home? **Sales Comparison.** 4 unit apartment? **Sales Comparison or GRM.** 50 unit apartment complex? **Income Approach.** Commercial Building? **Income Approach or GIM.** Church or Post Office? **Cost.**

o   What is the best way for a seller to determine the value of their property? Appraisal or CMA? **Appraisal.**

Pg. 56

o   Can an owner discriminate based upon a tenant's criminal history (drug dealing, violent history)? **Yes.**

o   Can an owner choose not to rent to a prospective tenant that is addicted to drugs, however is seeking treatment? **Yes.**

o   Can a landlord refuse to rent to an individual that has recovered from a mental issue? **Yes.**

o   In what manner can a landlord refuse to rent to family with children? **Max Occupancy Limits, 55+ Communities.**

o   Would a seller be liable for brokerage commission if they refuse to rent/sell property based upon a protected class? **Yes.**

- How many units can a property have and still qualify for an exemption under federal fair housing? **4**
- Would a landlord with a no pet policy need to rent to a tenant that has a comfort animal such as a dog, bird, or snake? **No.**
- Would a landlord be required to make an accommodation for a tenant that develops a handicap during tenancy? **No.** What if the handicap is for someone that moves in with the tenant (assuming it does not violate local occupancy regulations)? **No.**

1) An investor purchased a duplex in an area that permitted multi-family housing in 2000. On June 1, 2013 the county changed the zoning for the area to single family residential. Which of the following statements is TRUE?

    1.) The owner must obtain a variance to continue to use the home as a duplex.

    2.) The owner will have to stop using the property as a duplex and reset the home as a single family.

    3.) The owner may continue the use of the property as a duplex as this is a legal non-conforming use.

    4.) The owner must obtain a special use permit to continue to use the home as a duplex.

2) An agent is trying to determine the probable selling price for a property using the sales comparison approach. The subject property is inferior as it does not have a deck however the comparable property does. A deck is valued at $4,000. Which of the following adjustments should be made?

    1.) The comparable property should be adjusted downward.

    2.) The comparable property should be adjusted upward.

    3.) The subject property should be adjusted downward

    4.) The subject property should be adjusted upward.

3) In order to form a legally binding contract for real property, all of the following must occur, EXCEPT:

    1.) unconditional acceptance of the offer.

    2.) written agreement signed by all owners.

    3.) notification of acceptance.

    4.) delivery and acceptance of the signed offer.

4) The Seller agreed to deliver a General Warranty Deed to the Buyer. Which of the following is FALSE?

    1.) The Seller is obligated to defend the title against third party claims of ownership based upon past activity.

    2.) The General Warranty Deed provides the most protection to a purchaser.

    3.) Most standard offer to purchase forms used by brokers require the seller to provide the buyer a general warranty deed.

    4.) The General Warranty Deed automatically transfers marketable title to the Buyer.

    No why we have title ins.

5) Which of the following statements about option agreements is NOT correct?

    1.) The seller is obligated to check with the option holder prior to selling the property to another.

    2.) An option is a unilateral contract until exercised and then becomes a bilateral contract.

    3.) All of the terms about the purchase of the property are agreed to at the time the option agreement is signed.

    4.) The option automatically terminates when the option expires.

6) Which of the following is/are TRUE regarding disclosure?

I. The buyer's agent must disclose their agency status to the Seller or Seller's Agent at initial contact.

II. First substantial contact only occurs at face to face meetings.

　1.) I only
　2.) II only
　3.) Both I and II
　4.) Neither I nor II

7) "A" is purchasing a property from "B". The listing agent discovers that a relative of "B" may have an interest in the property. Which of the following is/are correct?

I. The Buyer cannot sue for Specific Performance as the relative is not a party to the contract.

II. The Seller should contact an attorney to try and obtain a quitclaim deed from the relative.

　1.) I only
　2.) II only
　(3.) Both I and II
　4.) Neither I nor II

8) Which of the following loans is not covered by the Truth-in-Lending Act?

　1.) Home Equity Line of Credit
　2.) Commercial Real Estate Loan
　3.) First Mortgage Loan
　4.) Second Mortgage Loan

9) A provisional broker is working for a buyer that becomes interested in a home that is also listed with the firm. All of the following types of agency may be permissible, EXCEPT

　1.) Designated
　2.) Dual
　3.) Exclusive
　4.) Special

10) A property has been under contract for 3 weeks and the due diligence period is set to expire in the next 48 hours. The buyer is requesting a 1 week extension. If the seller agrees to modify the contract and all parties initial and date the changes, which of the following have occurred?

1.) Substitution

2.) Novation
3.) Condemnation
4.) Amendment

11) Oscar agrees to purchase Emanuel's home for $140,000, with closing set for 60 days following the effective date of contract. Prior to the settlement date, Emanuel learns that Oscar is a minor. Based on this fact, the contract is now:

1.) valid.
2.) voidable.
3.) Void
4.) invalid.

12) Which of the following would typically increase a buyer's equity in the property?

I. An addition to the property to add a playroom and garage when paid for in cash.

II. A larger down payment at initial purchase.

1.) I only
2.) II only
3.) Both I and II
4.) Neither I nor II

13) Which of the following is/are TRUE with regard to contract formation?

I. The buyer or seller can opt to electronically sign contract forms and it is just as binding as a handwritten signature.

II. An option agreement is considered to be a unilateral contract until the option is exercised.

1.) I Only
2.) II Only
3.) Both I and II
4.) Neither I nor II

14) A minor desires to purchase real property, however her guardian has moved out of the state and relinquished her duties to act on the minor's behalf. The minor asked his school principal to sign the contract for him. The principal agreed and the agent, upon review of the signed offer stated that the property is "under contract". Which of the following statements is Correct?

1.) The contract is voidable as the intended owner is a minor.

2.) The contract is unenforceable as the principal did not have the authority to act on the minors behalf.

3.) The contract is enforceable against the property owner and the minor.

4.) The contract is valid against the property owner and the agent.

15) Lori, through her buyer's agent, submits an offer to purchase a property contingent upon her ability to obtain financing. The contingency date is 30 days and settlement date 45 days from the effective date of contract. Two days prior to the contingency expiration the lender notifies the buyer that they need an additional 7 days to complete the loan. In this circumstance, the seller:

1.) must grant the buyer an extension for the financing contingency and settlement date.

2.) must renegotiate the financing contingency date but not the settlement date.

3.) can automatically terminate the contract as the buyer is in breach for failing to obtain a loan by t contingency date.

4.) may retain the earnest money deposit if the bank denies the loan after the original loan contingency date.

16) A buyer is purchasing a property for $380,000 with a $2,000 initial earnest money deposit and $3,000 additional earnest money deposit. The buyer does not have the additional earnest money and the drop dead date is approaching. The buyer seeks to give the Seller a promissory note for the $3,000. Which of the following is true?

1.) The promissory note is a separate legal agreement from the mortgage financing.

2.) The lender would not want a copy of the promissory note to determine the buyer's qualification.

3.) The promissory note is a form of secured financing.

4.) A buyer can never sign a promissory note as earnest money.

17) Which of the following would be an example of mortgage fraud?

I. That a seller is providing a purchase money mortgage.

II. The lender calls the seller to seek a change in the purchase price to assist the buyer in qualifying.

1.) I only
2.) II only
3.) Both I and II
4.) Neither I nor II

18) All of the following statements are true regarding VA Loans, EXCEPT?

1.) The loans are guaranteed by the Government based upon a sliding scale.
2.) The loans have a higher loan to value than conventional financing.
3.) The interest rates are set by the lending institution.
4.) The loans are not assumable by non-veterans.

19) All of the following are true regarding RESPA (Real Estate Settlement Procedures Act), EXCEPT?

1.) Applies to mortgage loans made by banks with federally insured deposits.
2.) Applies to initial financing of residential properties.
3.) Informs buyers and sellers about all of the settlement costs.
4.) Regulates all real estate purchases.

20) Which of the following is/are true regarding property ownership?

I. Tenant in Common ownership may be acquired at the same time, from the same sources, at the same level of ownership.

II. Co-tenants with equal shares, purchased at the same time, from the same source with interest passing to their heirs upon death is Joint Tenancy.

1.) I only
2.) II only
3.) Both I and II
4.) Neither I nor II

21) Which of the following violate(s) a listing agent's duties to her principal?

   I. The listing agent discloses that the buyer is prequalified for an amount greater than the offer price.

   II. The listing agent fails to disclose to the buyer that the seller is currently delinquent on his mortgage.

   1.) I only
   2.) II only
   3.) Both I and II
   4.) Neither I nor II

22) All of the following are TRUE regarding police powers EXCEPT:

   1.) The property owner is compensated based on the tax value of the property if their property is condemned.
   2.) Eminent domain is the right to take property for the public good.
   3.) Building codes and environmental laws are forms of police power.
   4.) When an owner dies without heirs, the property escheats to the state.

23) The contract between a buyer and seller for the purchase of real property is considered a(n):

   1.) voidable contract.
   2.) bilateral contract.
   3.) unilateral contract.
   4.) conditional contract.

24) Which of the following statements is/are CORRECT regarding a minor that leases an apartment?

   I. The minor cannot terminate the lease agreement once they reach the age of majority.

   II. An agreement with a minor regarding real estate is void. *it's voidable*

   1.) I only.
   2.) II only.
   3.) Both I and II.
   4.) Neither I nor II.

25) A property manager is preparing an operating budget for the owner. Which of the following would have the LEAST weight when selecting the rental rates for the apartments?

Current Market

    1.) The vacancy rate of comparable properties.

    ↘2.) The amount the owner needs to cover debt service.

    3.) The rental rates for comparable properties with similar units.

    4.) The current absorption in the local rental market.

vacancy to occupied

26) John hired Kelly, a provisional broker affiliated with ABC Realty, to list his home located in a quiet neighborhood. The area is desirable and both anticipate significant interest in the property. Which of the following listing agreements would not require John to pay Kelly's firm in the event that John locates the buyer?

    1.) Exclusive Right to Sell Listing Agreement

    ↘ 2.) Exclusive Agency Listing Agreement

    3.) Net Listing Agreement

    4.) Full Service Listing Agreement

27) J makes an offer to purchase a property on Monday at 5 PM for $425,000 with the Seller paying $5,000 in closing cost and closing within 45 days. The Seller agrees to all the terms except for the days to close, changing it to 30 days and returning it to J at 4 PM on Tuesday. On Wednesday at 3 PM J initials and dates the change and emails his agent. Which of the following statements is correct?

    (1.) A legally binding contract has not yet been formed.

    2.) A legally binding contract was formed when J signed and emailed the agreement.

    ✗3.) A counter-offer occurred when the buyer initialed the agreement.

    4.) A legally binding contract was formed at 4 PM on Tuesday.

28) All of the following are CORRECT with regards to a tenant security/pet deposit EXCEPT:

    1.) The Owner cannot charge more than 2 months of security deposit for a 6 month lease.

    (2.) The Owner can charge damage costs against the security deposit when it occurs.

    3.) The Owner is entitled to charge a 2 week deposit if the rental is week to week.

    ↘4.) The Owner cannot charge a pet deposit for a service animal.

29) Which of the following is/are true regarding fixtures?

I. A hot tub that has been wired and plumbed into a home would be considered a fixture.

II. The restaurant equipment left after the tenant has vacated is no longer considered a trade fixture.

    1.) I only.
    2.) II only.
    3.) Both I and II.
    4.) Neither I nor II.

30) Which of the following statements is/are true regarding financing?

I. In order to avoid private mortgage insurance, a lender may require a buyer to have at least a 20% down payment.

II. VA and FHA financing does not permit prepayment penalties.

    1.) I only.
    2.) II only.
    3.) Both I and II.
    4.) Neither I nor II.

31) All of the following are permitted to be included in a listing agreement between a seller and a brokerage firm, EXCEPT:

    1.) the beginning date, agreed upon marketing date and expiration date of the contract.
    2.) a disclaimer of liability for the brokerage when an affiliated broker makes an error advertising the property on the MLS or other internet media.
    3.) the authority for broker to disclose the existence of other offers on the property.
    4.) the terms and conditions upon which compensation will be earned.

32) During a preliminary walk through of a home the seller told the listing agent that the roof leaks during heavy rain. The listing agent made a note of this fact in his file but failed to make any further inquiry. At an open house a prospective buyer asked if there were any issues that would require immediate repair, to which the listing agent said no. The prospective buyer purchased the home without an inspection. Two weeks after closing the buyer noticed a leak and was shocked to discover extensive water damage to the ceiling. Which of the following is TRUE?

   1.) The listing agent is not liable as the buyer failed to order a property inspection.
   2.) The listing agent is guilty of negligent omission.
   3.) The Seller is responsible for the listing agent's actions through subrogation.
   4.) The listing agent is guilty of willful misrepresentation.

33) Which of the following statements is/are TRUE with regard to an exclusive right to represent the buyer in a purchase transaction.

I. The buyer's broker may also be referred to as the selling broker in an offer to purchase.

II. The buyer's broker is entitled to the compensation outlined in the exclusive right to represent the buyer no matter how the buyer was introduced to the property that they decide to purchase.

   1.) I only
   2.) II only
   3.) Both I and II
   4.) Neither I nor II

34) Which of the following best describes multiple owners of an entity where some are passive investors that have limited liability and no direct say in the operations of the organization?

   1.) C-Corporation
   2.) S-Corporation
   3.) Restricted Proprietorship
   4.) Limited Partnership

35) Terry owns a property that is located near a major university. He anticipates that property values will appreciate significantly over the next few years so rather than selling the property, he decides to rent it out. Which of the following statements is correct?

   1.) Terry has a leasehold interest in the property and has given up the right of control.
   2.) Terry has a leasehold interest in the property and has given up the right of possession.
   3.) Terry has a leased fee interest in the property and has given up the right of control.
   4.) Terry has a leased fee interest in the property and has given up the right of possession.

36) How is loan to value calculated when a borrower obtains conventional financing?

      1.) Desired loan divided by a thousand and multiplied by the amortization rate.

      2.) Mortgage amount divided by the lesser of the appraised value or contract price.

      3.) Appraised value multiplied by the mortgage amount.

      4.) Desired loan multiplied by the down payment.

37) Which of the following statements is FALSE regarding property management?

      1.) An unlicensed assistant to a property manager can fill in pre-printed forms and show property to prospective tenants.

      2.) A license is not required if an officer of a Corporation is leasing property for the Corporations benefit.

      3.) There is no exemption for Federal Fair Housing if the owner is renting a property with 5 or more units.

      4.) A real estate licensee may prepare commercial leases for multiple properties even if each propert requires unique terms.

38) Shelly purchases a beach property where she owns the unit itself as well as co-ownership of the common areas. Shelly owns:

      1.) a townhouse.

      2.) a co-op.

      3.) a condo.

      4.) a planned unit.

39) Which of the following statements is/are true with regard to agency agreements?

I. Agency is not formed until the Firm signs the listing or buyer agency agreement.

II. All agency agreements must be reduced to writing at their inception.

      1.) I only.

      2.) II only.

      3.) Both I and II.

      4.) Neither I nor II.

40) K submits an offer to L at 3 PM on Thursday. L agrees to all terms but increases the earnest money by $500 at 6 PM on Thursday then signs and delivers the document to K's agent. K makes a counteroffer and sends it back to L's agent. On Friday at 9 AM L receives the agreement from her agent. At 10 AM Friday L signs and sends the document back to K through email. Which of the following statements is TRUE?

I. A legally binding contract was formed at 10 AM Friday.

II. L would not be able to automatically cancel the agreement if K has not delivered the earnest money.

   1.) I only.
   2.) II only.
   3.) Both I and II.
   4.) Neither I nor II.

41) Which of the following best describes when a bank demands immediate payment of the entire loan balance due to a default by the borrower?

   1.) Subordination
   2.) Acceleration
   3.) Due on Sale
   4.) Demand on Default

42) Which of the following is FALSE with regard to mortgage financing?

   1.) The risk of default is higher for adjustable rate mortgages than fixed mortgages.
   2.) A borrower often pays discount points to lower the interest rate stated on the bank note.
   3.) Construction loans are the most risky and often require a borrower to obtain a "take-out commitment".
   4.) A borrower with limited funds to purchase would seek a blanket loan which allows a parent to cosign on the mortgage.

43) A single family home has lost value as a result of the area becoming more commercial rather than residential. This is an example of:

   1.) Functional Obsolescence
   2.) Highest and Best Use
   3.) Conformity
   4.) Economic Obsolescence

44) A buyer agrees to purchase a property, with the seller providing financing through a contract for deed. Which of the following statements is/are CORRECT?

I. The buyer is referred to as the vendee and will hold equitable title in the property until final payment.

II. The seller is referred to as the vendor is entitled to sue the buyer for a deficiency judgment in the event of default.

1.) I Only
2.) II Only
3.) Both I and II
4.) Neither I nor II

45) Eric desires to purchase a property by investing an inheritance and obtaining a new loan. He asks his broker to explain the lending process. Which of the following statements by the agent is FALSE?

1.) An extender clause in a mortgage permits a borrower to lock in an interest rate for a specific peri of time.

2.) The loan origination fee charged by a lender covers the administrative costs of making a loan.

3.) A lender will require account statements to confirm the borrower's assets from checking, savings and investment accounts.

4.) The lender will review the debt to service ratio to determine the borrower's credit worthiness.

46) A brokerage has an in-house mortgage lender and title insurance company. The owner of the brokerage requires that a licensee recommend the use of both to all buyers. Which of the following statements is correct?

1.) The broker should recommend only these companies as instructed by the owner.
✓2.) The broker should recommend both service providers, disclosing the brokerage interest, and other service providers to the buyer.
3.) The broker should recommend both companies and refer the buyer to an attorney should they have any questions.
4.) The broker would be in violation of Commission rules if they recommend these companies under any circumstance.

47) Which of the following is/are correct regarding ad valorem property taxes?

   I. They are always charged on manufactured homes.

   II. Are authorized to be charged by a county under the machinery act.

   1.) I only
   2.) II only
   3.) Both I and II
   4.) Neither I nor II

48) Which of the following would be considered a material fact that must be disclosed to a prospective buyer?

   1.) The seller is behind on his mortgage.
   2.) The previous owner died from complications of AIDs.
   3.) The seller purchased the property at a foreclosure auction.
   4.) A methamphetamine lab had been in the house.

49) A provisional broker working for an owner under a property management agreement is authorized to do which of the following on behalf of the owner?

   1.) Bind the principal to all contracts.
   2.) Make improvements designed to increase the property value and charge the owner.
   3.) Authorize the repair of a burst pipe without the consent of the owner. *Can protect property*
   4.) Place the security deposit into the brokerage account.

   Trust or escrow → SD

50) An owner has agreed to an option to purchase her property. Which of the following is TRUE?

   1.) The option must be exercised during the option period.
   2.) The purchase price is determined when the option is exercised.
   3.) In order for the owner to sell the property they must first present the offer to the option holder who must elect to buy the property or release the option.
   4.) The option holder is not obligated to purchase the property.

51) A large home is surrounded by smaller, less expensive homes. The value of the larger home

      1.) will increase as it has more square footage than nearby homes.

      2.) will not be affected by the smaller nearby homes.

      3.) will have a diminished value per square foot compared to the smaller homes.

      4.) will increase in value by a large percentage because it is larger than nearby homes.

52) Which of the following is/are required under the Federal Fair Housing Act of 1988?

      I. A handicap tenant is permitted to widen doorways, install pull bars and a wheelchair ramp at his own expense.

      II. There is no exception for a seller that owns 5 single family homes for discrimination based upon the protected classes

      1.) I only

      2.) II only

      3.) Both I and II

      4.) Neither I nor II

53) All of the following are true regarding the 1968 Federal Fair Housing Act Except:

      1.) A religious organization that rents units at a reduced rate for the benefit of their membership is exempt.

      2.) Complaints are filed with HUD within 1 year from the incident and HUD has 100 days to respond.

      3.) Familial status refers to families with children under the age of 18 and pregnant women.

      4.) An owner occupant that refuses to rent a unit in a quadplex based on the prospective tenants race would violate the act even if they did not use discriminatory advertising.

54) Which of the following is/are required to form a legally binding contract to purchase real estate?

      I. Earnest Money

      II. Acknowledgement

      1.) I Only

      2.) II Only

      3.) Both I and II

      4.) Neither I nor II

National Practice Exam 1

55) A broker will violate the Sherman Antitrust Act in which of the following scenarios?

I. A broker refuses to work with a particular home inspector even if the client requests to use the home inspector.

II. A broker does not disclose a referral fee he paid to an out of state broker to a prospective buyer client.

   1.) I Only
   2.) II Only
   3.) Both I and II
   4.) Neither I nor II

56) A salesperson would violate the Do Not Call law in which of the following situations, when the property owner has placed his/her contact phone number on the Do Not Call registry?

   1.) The salesperson calls the owner of a home whose listing agreement expired 15-months ago when the property had been listed by another broker affiliated with the firm.
   2.) The salesperson calls an owner of an expired property that he met while holding an open house at a neighboring property, where the expired owner gave permission to call.
   3.) The salesperson calls an owner of a property whose listing agreement expired 17-months ago which was listed by a different company than the salesperson is affiliated with. *Someone else*
   4.) The salesperson calls a For Sale By Owner to inquire about the property price and whether the owner will pay commission to a buyers agent.

57) Which of the following would tend to increase property values?

   1.) A large employer relocates into the city that the property is located.
   2.) The number of homes on the market increases.
   3.) Interest rates rise sharply.
   4.) A refinery opens beside a residential neighborhood.

58) Which of the following would violate state or federal law?

I. Sending unsolicited emails without telling recipients how to opt out of receiving future emails.

II. Sending unsolicited mail through the US Postal Service.

   1.) I only
   2.) II only
   3.) Both I and II
   4.) Neither I nor II

59) A borrower defaulted on a mortgage in a title theory state. The lender held a foreclosure auction, and the property sold for less than the amount currently owed to the bank. Which of the following statements is FALSE?

   1.) The borrower has the statutory right of redemption, giving them 10-days to redeem the property by paying the full amount due.
   2.) The lender may be able to sue for a deficiency judgment if the amount obtained at the auction is less that the amount owed by the borrower.
   3.) The lender must continue to auction the property until a higher bid is placed over the amount owed by the borrower.
   4.) The property is typically transferred by a trustee's deed to the highest bidder at the auction.

60) Which of the following statements is/are correct with regard to Title Insurance Policies?

I. A borrower will pay for the policy at the time of closing and must renew the owners' policy on a yearly basis to maintain coverage.

II. An extended policy covers unrecorded rights of persons in possession, survey errors and unrecorded liens not known by the policy holder.

   a) I Only
   b) II Only
   c) Both I and II
   d) Neither I nor II

61) Which of the following would terminate an Exclusive Right to Sell Listing Agreement in a multi-broker firm?

I. The death or insanity of a provisional broker that signed the agreement.

II. The broker that signed the agreement resigns and affiliates with another brokerage.

   1.) I only
   2.) II only
   3.) Both I and II
\ 4.) Neither I nor II

62) Ben is managing a commercial property for Kelly where the tenant will pay a monthly rent plus taxes, insurance and common area maintenance. Which lease type is being offered?

   1.) Gross Lease
   2.) Percentage Lease
`3.) Net Lease
   4.) Ground Lease

63) All of the following would be a legal basis for rejecting a rental application EXCEPT:

   1.) The prospective tenant's family is too large for the apartment to accommodate.
   2.) The prospective tenant was evicted from a previous apartment 6 years ago.
   \3.) The prospective tenant has small children and the available unit is located near a retired couple, one of whom is undergoing chemotherapy.
   4.) The prospective tenant has too many monthly recurring debt obligations making timely rental payment very difficult.

64) A broker that is representing a property owner through a valid property management agreement will typically be authorized to perform which of the following tasks?

I. Make improvements to the property that the broker believes will increase the rent that can be charged each month.

II. Pay for replacing an HVAC system at a cost of $5,000 from trust account funds when the trust account balance is $100,000 and the clients repair reserve account balance is $4,500.

    1.) I Only

    2.) II Only

    3.) Both I and II

    • 4.) Neither I nor II

65) Which of the following financial regulations require the disclosure of the financing terms when a trigger term is used?

    1.) Real Estate Settlement Procedures Act

    ~ 2.) Regulation Z

    3.) Truth in Lending

    4.) Financial Reform Act of 2009

no dual

66) The listing agent receives a call from a prospective buyer that is interested in the property. The Seller has only agreed to (exclusive) representation and will not give permission to represent the buyer in any capacity. Assuming the buyer agrees to represent themselves in the transaction which of the following statements is TRUE?

    ↘ 1.) The listing agent is not required to determine if the home will meet all of the buyer's needs, unle the buyer discloses his/her proposed use and then needs to instruct the buyer to verify the possibility or refer the buyer to an attorney.

    2.) The listing agent can prepare a comparative market analysis for the buyer so long as it does not provide for a specific offer price, only a range of value.

    3.) The listing agent can disclose to the buyer that the seller will accept less than the offer price if in fact the seller is willing to accept less.

    4.) The prospective buyer is owed honesty, fairness and disclosure of seller's reason for moving.

67) Which of the following best describes a licensee that shows a prospective buyer neighborhoods based upon the buyer's color rather than on the amenities of the homes?

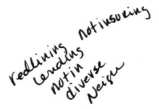

redlining not insuring
Lending not in
diverse Neigh

   1.) Redlining

   2.) Blockbusting

   ↘3.) Steering

   4.) Misdirection

68) All of the following are CORRECT with regards to lead based paint EXCEPT:

   1.) The buyer should be given the pamphlet "Protecting Your Family From Lead in the Home".

   2.) Encapsulation is the primary method to protect against the hazards of lead based paint.

   3.) The buyer is allowed an opportunity to inspect the home for lead based paint.

   ↘4.) The Lead Based Paint Addendum must be used if the home was built prior to 1992.

69) Which of the following statements is/are true regarding a purchase contract for real property?

I. A contract that has not closed is considered executory. T

II. The buyer has an equitable interest in the property until the purchase is completed. T

   1.) I only.

   2.) II only.

   ↘3.) Both I and II.

   4.) Neither I nor II.

70) A party meets all the statutory requirements to take an acre tract of land. Which of the following best describes the legal action that will be taken?

   1.) Adverse Possession

   ↘2.) Suit to Quiet Title

   3.) Right of Redemption

   4.) Eminent Domain

71) Which of the following statements is/are TRUE regarding agency agreements?

I. A Power of Attorney is considered special agency representation of a principal.

II. The Exclusive Right to Represent Buyer is a general agency representation agreement.

    1.) I only.
    2.) II only.
    3.) Both I and II.
    ` 4.) Neither I nor II.

72) Which of the following best describes the action an individual homeowner in a neighborhood with restrictive covenants would take when a neighbor is violating the covenants?

    1.) File a complaint with the local housing department.
    2.) Encourage neighbors to send letters demanding the neighbor to stop.
    3.) Contact the Police in order to lodge a complaint.
    ` 4.) Seek an injunction through the courts.

73) Which of the following defines when a lien with a higher priority takes a lower position?

    `1.) Subordination
    2.) Refinancing
    3.) Disintermediation
    4.) Affirmation

74) Which of the following statements is/are TRUE with regard to providing an adequate legal description of a property in a contract?

I. The metes and bounds property descriptions is the primary method used in the US.

II. Reference to recorded documents such as plat book and page and deed book and page are sufficier to uniquely identify a property.

    1.) I only
    ` 2.) II only
    3.) Both I and II
    4.) Neither I nor II

75) Which of the following would have the greatest impact on the establishment of a listing price?

    1.) A similar home that sold FSBO

    2.) The current condition of the market

    3.) The Seller's desire to net $50,000

    4.) The sale of similar property in the past 12 months

76) Which of the following statements is/are TRUE with regard to the duties owed to customers and clients?

I. A licensee owes a customer honesty, fairness and negotiation.

II. A licensee owes a client loyalty and honesty.

    1.) I only

    2.) II only

    3.) Both I and II

    4.) Neither I nor II

77) A property is foreclosed upon to satisfy a lien. Which of the following would generally have the least priority?

    1.) Property Taxes

    2.) Mechanics Lien

    3.) First Mortgage

    4.) Federal Income Tax or State

78) Which of the following leases are commonly used for retail tenants?

    1.) Full Lease

    2.) Gross Lease

    3.) Net Lease

    4.) Percentage Lease

79) Which of the following statements is/are TRUE regarding the income capitalization approach?

I. Net operating income is calculated by taking the effective gross income and subtracting operating expenses and vacancy losses.

II. The capitalization rate is determined by taking the selling price of other buildings and dividing by the gross market rent.

    1.) I only

    2.) II only

    3.) Both I and II

    4.) Neither I nor II

80) The property manager signed a lease for 2 weeks that renewed for successive periods unless 15 days notice is provided by either party. This is an example of:

    1.) Estate for Years

    2.) Estate from Year to Year

    3.) Estate at Condition

    4.) Estate at Notice

81) The owner of a property desires to change the zoning of a large tract of land into a subdivision that wil provide affordable housing. The owner did not have to go through the typical process to obtain approval. The owner received a:

    1.) Variance Permit.

    2.) Spot Zoning Permit.

    3.) Subsequent Exception Permit.

    4.) Special Use Permit.

82) A licensee is contacted by two brothers seeking to sell a home that they recently inherited. Which of the following statements is/are TRUE?

I. The licensee should contact the decedent's attorney for a copy of the release of title.

II. The licensee should verify the owner of record.

    1.) I only

    2.) II only

    3.) Both I and II

    4.) Neither I nor II

83) Which of the following statements is FALSE regarding commissions?

    1.) The Real Estate Commission does not hear complaints regarding compensation between brokers.

    2.) Commission is negotiable and not charged based on a "going rate".

    \3.) The Seller can reduce the commission rate if the home does not sell for a high enough price.

    4.) In the event that a Seller refuses to pay a commission upon settlement and closing, the agent cannot recommend that the Buyer terminate the contract.

84) All of the following statements are true concerning deed restrictions EXCEPT:

    1.) They are binding on current and future owners of the property.

    \2.) They are enforced through the courts upon complaint to the sheriff's department

    3.) They are typically more restrictive than zoning laws and regulations.

    4.) They may result in the loss of the property when the restriction is violated.

85) A seller has agreed to pay 6% commission to the listing firm. The seller has a loan balance of $125,000 and other closing costs paid by the seller of $1,400. The closing is scheduled for October 18th and taxes of $1,381 have been paid for the year. The following expenses were paid by the customary party – deed preparation - $125, courier fee for loan documents - $35, title insurance $270 and closing fee $600. What does the sales price need to be in order for the seller to net $30,000 rounded to the nearest hundred?

    1.) $165,600

    \2.) $166,200

    3.) $166,600

    4.) $167,200

Handwritten work:

Known exp   125,000
        + 1400.00
        − 276.26
        + 125
        + 30,000
        156 248 ÷ 94% =
        166,222.12

D b
Cr S

1381 ÷ 360 × 72
= 276.20

86) X owns a property with 187,500 square feet and a depth of 250'. X purchased an adjoining lot located on the same street with 112,500 square feet and a depth of 250'. What is the total street frontage that X now owns?

    \1.) 1,200'

    2.) 1,000'

    3.) 700'

    4.) 500'

Handwritten work:

187500 ÷ 250 = 750

112500 ÷ 250 = 450

1200 front foot

87) A prospective seller owns a property that measures 4,500' X 1,800'. A similar property recently sold for $45,000 per acre. What is the probable selling price for the seller's property?

1.) $ 192,086

2.) $ 5,695,312

| 3.) $ 8,367,768

4.) $69,034,090

$4500 \times 1800 = 8,100,000$

$\div 43560 = 185.950$

$8,367,768.4$

88) A bank limits lending to 3 times the applicant's gross income. A couple has $45,000 as a down payment and wants to purchase a home for $315,000. What is the minimum yearly income the couple would need in order to qualify?

$315000 - 45,000 = 270,000 \div 3 \neq 90,000$

1.) $ 75,000

/2.) $ 90,000

3.) $100,000

4.) $105,000

89) A property is located in a county that determines the assessed value to be 70% of the fair market value. The county charges 18 mills. The fair market value of the property is $280,000. What is the monthly tax burden?

$196,000 \div 1000 \times 18$

$tax \div (AV \div 1000) = mills$

/1.) $ 294

2.) $ 420

3.) $3,528

4.) $5,040

90) The listing agreement calls for a listing price of $250,000 and 8% commission to be split between the listing and selling agent. The agent representing the buyer submits an offer for $240,000 but later accepts the seller's counteroffer of $245,000. The selling agent's independent contractor agreement calls for a 70/30 split between the agent and the brokerage. Upon closing how much will the selling agent be paid?

$245,000 \times 4\% = 9800 \times 70\% = 6860$

1.) $ 6,720

| 2.) $ 6,860

3.) $ 7,000

4.) $19,600

91) An investor purchased a 4 acre tract of land for $75,000. She subdivides the lot into 8 lots for resale at $35,000 each. What was the approximate percentage of gross profit that the investor earned?

1.) 2.73%

2.) 27%

√3.) 273%

4.) 373%

New ÷ old ÷ old

N/0 ÷ 0   280,000 - 75,000 ÷ 75,000 = 2.733 = 273%

35,000 × 8

92) An apartment complex has effective gross income $120,000 with a vacancy and collection loss of 5%. The owner has the following expenses: $10,000 management fee, $15,000 debt service, $5,000 depreciation and $8,000 in other operating expenses. What is the value of the building if the owner capitalization rate is 15%

1.) $607,000

2.) $640,000

3.) $680,000

4.) $800,000

NOI ÷ Rate = value

CAP Rate

93) A property has a fair market value of $200,000 located outside North Carolina. The assessed value is $175,000. What is the approximate mills tax rate if the monthly tax liability is $217.30?

1.) 1.30

2.) 1.49

3.) 13.0

↘4.) 14.9

217.30 × 12

2607.6

2607.6 ÷ (175000 ÷ 1000)
            175   14.9

94) What is the living area square footage of the one story property illustrated below?

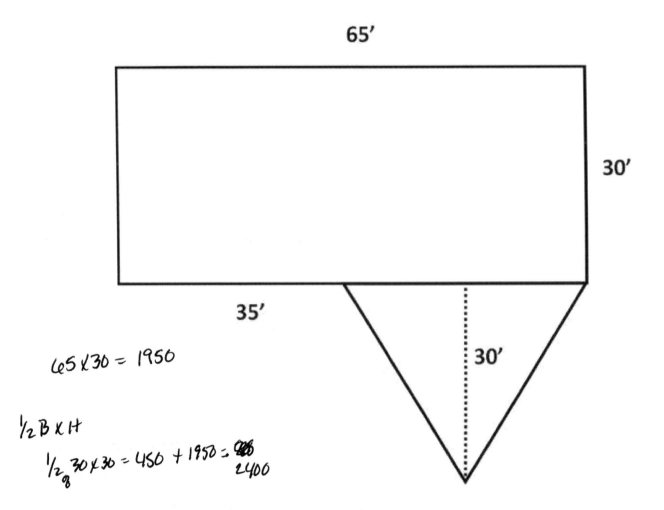

65'

30'

35'

30'

$65 \times 30 = 1950$

$\frac{1}{2} B \times H$

$\frac{1}{2} 30 \times 30 = 450 + 1950 = \cancel{2405}$
2400

1.) 1,950
2.) 2,400
3.) 2,725
4.) 2,850

95) A licensee is using the cost approach to value a property that is 4,500 square feet and a replacement cost of $110 per square foot. The building was built 10 years ago, has an economic life of 75 years and an effective age of 5 years. A lot similar to the subject property recently sold for $55,000. The probable sales price of the property would be rounded to the nearest $1,000?

1.) $429,000
2.) $462,000
3.) $484,000
4.) $517,000

$N - D + L +$
$N - Dep + L + improvents$
$New - Depriciation + Land + improve$

$495,000 \div 75 \times 5$
$SP \div Econ life \times effive age$

Gross Rent Mult.

96) An investor purchased a property for $180,000 that is a residential tri-plex. The units rent for $750 each per month. Based upon the information above what would the monthly gross rent multiplier be?

1.) 0.125

2.) 1.25

3.) 80.0

4.) 240.0

GRM   SP ÷ MR

750 × 3

Sale price ÷ Monthly Rent

180,000 ÷ 2250

97) A buyer couple wants to purchase a home with a loan of $360,000 at 6% interest. The principal and interest payment will be $2,150. In addition the couple's yearly property tax liability will be $7,200 and monthly insurance will be $50. The couple has a monthly car payment of $650 and a $50 student loan (that matures in 5 months). The couple earns $150,000 per year. What is the maximum monthly debt obligations the couple can have in addition to the ones listed above and still qualify for conventional financing?

1.) $1,000

2.) $1,050

3.) $1,700

4.) $4,500

H
2150
+ 600
+ 50
2800
3500

TD
2800
+ 650
3450

= 4500 - 3450 = 1050

7200 ÷ 12 = 600

PITI 2800

150,000 ÷ 12 = 12500
X

98) A property manager is trying to determine the annual rent per unit rounded to the nearest $10 if a property has 100 units and the following income and expenses:

Before tax cash flow $750,000
Property Taxes $ 50,000
Management Fees $100,000
Depreciation $ 25,000
Debt Service $ 75,000
Vacancy & Collection 5%

1.) $ 860

2.) $ 880

3.) $10,260

4.) $10,530

1026375.70 ÷ 100 units

GI 100%
5% 95%÷   95?
- VC   975,000
EGI
-op ek   *5000 100,000*
NOI   *50,000*
- Dept   *+ 75,000*
BTCF   *750,000*

No Dept Ser
C upinprou
Depriciation

99) Paul agreed to sell his property for $300,000, with the closing scheduled for October 23rd. Paul's mortgage payoff on the day of closing is $199,800. The following expenses will be paid by the customary party:

* Mortgage Cancellation Fee $45 * Commission 7% * Deed Preparation $125
* Closing Attorney Fee $800 * Deed Recording Fee $45 * Other Seller Closing Costs $4,000
* Property Taxes Paid In Advance of Closing by Seller - $4,780, with buyer paying
  tax beginning on the day of closing

How much will the seller net from the sale of the property, rounded to the nearest dollar?

1.) $75,946

2.) $75,933

3.) $74,140

4.) $74,127

(handwritten:
300,000
− 198 800
45.00
125
4000
)

100) A buyer is purchasing a property for $180,000 by obtaining a conventional mortgage with 90% loan to value for 20 year at 3.75% interest. The buyer paid $3,000 as an earnest money deposit, which the closing attorney deposited into his escrow account. Closing is scheduled for March 4th. The following expenses were paid by the customary party at closing:

* 1% Origination Fee * 2% Discount Points * Deed Preparation $150
* Prepaid / Interim Interest * Closing Attorney Fee $850 * Appraisal Fee $400 (paid at mortgage application)
* Property Taxes $1,800, unpaid and buyer to pay property taxes beginning on the day of closing.

How much will the buyer pay on the day of closing to purchase the home, rounded to the nearest dollar?

1.) $21,251

2.) $20,846

3.) $20,834

4.) $20,801

1.   3 – When a municipality changes the zoning classification, properties that were legally operating in the past may continue their use, even though the property does not conform to the current zoning requirements. This is known as a legal nonconforming use. A variance is a minor change to minimize hardship, however is not used to maximize profit. In this example, the nonconforming use of the property as a duplex may continue. The owner would not be required to reset it is a single family property. A special use permit is granted when a property owner desires to use the property in a manner that is in the public interest such as a museum, hospital or church.

2.   1 - When using the sales comparison approach is important to remember that you never adjust the subject property. One way to ensure this is to recall "comp superior subtract" and "comp inferior increase". When the subject property is inferior that means that the comparable property is superior, so the comparable property would be adjusted downward.

3.   4 - In order to form a legally binding contract there must be an offer, it must be in writing, signed by the parties with unconditional acceptance and notification of acceptance to the offeror. There is no requirement that the contract be delivered. Delivery and acceptance is a requirement for the essential elements of a valid deed not purchase contracts.

4.   4 – A general warranty deed is used to transfer ownership from grantor to grantee. It does not guarantee marketable title has been transferred to the buyer. This is why it is so important for a buyer to obtain title insurance. The grantor or seller would be required to defend the grantee or buyer against third-party claims of ownership.

5.   1 – Under an option agreement, the owner has tied up their property, preventing sale to another party until the option is exercised or expires. When a seller agrees to a right of first refusal, the seller would be obligated to check with party that contracted for the right before being able to sell the property to another. It is very important to remember that all terms of an option are agreed to up front including the purchase price, period of time to exercise, period of time to close and steps that must be taken to exercise.

6. 1 – A buyer's agent must inform the seller or sellers agent that they represent the buyer at initial contact. Initial contact may occur at any time up to presentation of an offer. First substantial contact is defined as the point in time where conversation shifts from facts about the property to personal and confidential information that could weaken a buyer or seller's bargaining position. This can occur in person, over the phone or in an email.

7. 3 - Since a relative is not a party to the contract, the buyer would not be able to sue for specific performance. Specific performance is forcing the seller to sell the property. One way of resolving this potential conflict is to have the relative sign a quit claim deed, quitting whatever claim they may or may not have to the property. This would be prepared by an attorney, not a broker.

8. 2 – The Truth-in-Lending Act applies to consumer finance including first mortgage, second mortgage and home equity lines of credit. It would not apply to commercial real estate loans, business loans or agricultural loans.

9. 3 – When a broker/brokerage represents the interest of one party it is known as exclusive agency. Dual agency arises when the buyer and seller are represented by the same firm, where the broker/brokerage is not permitted to advocate on behalf of one party over the other. Designated agency is a form of dual agency, where the brokerage represents both the buyer and seller, however the broker in charge appoints a broker to represent the buyer and another broker to represent seller. Under designated agency each broker is permitted to advocate on behalf of his or her client.

10. 4 – The agreement to modify a contract is known as an amendment. The term substitution relates to the valuation, where the property with the lowest price will sell the faster than a comparable property offered at a higher price. Novation is the act of replacing a party to the contract with the release of liability. Condemnation is part of police powers where property can be taken for the public good.

11. 2 - A minor can legally enter into a contract to purchase real estate. The contract is considered voidable, where the minor may terminate the contract without penalty. The adult is still obligated to perform under the terms of the contract.

12. 3 – Equity is defined as the difference between the fair market value of the property and the amount owed. Equity increases when a borrower makes additional principal payments, improves the property in a manner that increases its value, through appreciation or by making a larger initial down payment.

13. 3 – Under the Uniform Electronic Transactions Act a digital signature is just as binding as a wet pen signature. Option agreements are considered unilateral until exercised at which point it becomes a bilateral contract. The optionor/seller is bound to perform since they have granted the optionee/buyer an unrestricted and irrevocable option to purchase the property if the option is excised in the manner agreed to in the option contract.

14. 2 – A guardian may be appointed to handle the affairs of a minor. When the guardian is no longer able to perform, the courts must appoint a new party to act in that capacity. The high school principal lacks the capacity to act in this role without court appointment. The property is not under contract as a legally binding contract has not been formed.

15. 4 – The buyer and seller contractually agreed to the financing contingency. The buyer risks the loss of his or her earnest money deposit if the bank denies the loan after the original loan contingency date. The seller "may" but is not obligated to amend the contract to a later loan contingency date.

16. 1 – A promissory note is not the same as a mortgage. While it is very unlikely that a seller would agree to take back a promissory note in lieu of payment of an earnest money deposit, it is possible for the buyer to request it. The promissory note must be disclosed to the lender to avoid mortgage fraud.

17. 2 – The fact that a seller is providing some or all of the purchase price is not an indication of mortgage fraud. Straw buyers – using another person's social security number, lying about income / assets, contract kiting – two contracts, one sent to the bank and one at a lower amount that reflects the actual purchase price, false gift letters or a lender seeking a price change on behalf of the buyer are examples of loan fraud.

18. 4 – VA loans are assumable by veterans and nonveterans. Only a veteran with an entitlement or qualifying widow or widower can originate a VA loan. "We owe our veterans more" so VA loans are guaranteed not insured. The lender can charge origination fees and discount points. The loan is made by the lending institution but guaranteed by the VA.

19. 4 – The Real Estate Settlements Procedures Act applies to residential real estate purchases when a loan is involved. RESPA does not apply to commercial or business loans, vacant land sales where none of the proceeds will be used to construct a residential structure, large tracts of land of 25 acres or more and certain loan assumptions. RESPA does apply to federally related residential mortgages where the government insures or guarantees the loan, the bank is FDIC insured or the loan will be sold on the secondary market.

20. 1 - When multiple people own property as tenants in common they "may" have the same level of ownership or different levels of ownership. Under joint tenancy

property passes to the other co-owners rather than one's heirs. One way to remember this is that you do not pass a joint to your kids.

21. 4 – The listing agent has a duty to disclose all information that they learn about the buyer, even personal and confidential information that could weaken the buyers bargaining position. The listing agent represents the seller, not the buyer. A listing agent must disclose material facts to all parties involved in the transaction. It is not a material fact that the seller is behind of the mortgage unless foreclosure notice has been received.

22. 1 – If a municipality condemns a property through eminent domain, the owner is compensated for the fair market value of the property, not the tax value.

23. 2 – A bilateral contract is a mutual exchange of promises between two parties, where both have agreed to perform. In this circumstance the buyer agrees to buy and the seller agrees to sell the property. A unilateral contract only requires one party to perform if the other party acts. A voidable contract allows one party to proceed with or terminate the contract, while the other party is obligated to perform. Some examples of voidable contracts include contracts with a minor, default by the buyer or seller depending upon the contract, or damage to the property prior to closing in a real estate contract.

24. 4 – In many states a minor can terminate a contract within 12 months of reaching the age of majority. An agreement with a minor to purchase real estate is considered voidable on behalf of the minor. The adult will be required to perform.

25. 2 – Rental rates are determined based upon overall market conditions, not on the rate of return desired by the landlord/property owner. The amount of rent the seller can charge will be based on supply and demand, vacancy rates and rental rates of comparable properties.

26. 2 – When a seller lists the property with one brokerage and is able to compete with the brokerage to avoid paying commission, they have agreed to an exclusive agency listing agreement. Under an exclusive right to sell, no matter how the property is sold the brokerage will be paid. A net listing states that the broker will receive proceeds in excess of an agreed-upon net amount required by the seller.

27. 1 – In order to form a legally binding contract to purchase real estate, there must be a written offer that is accepted without change and then communication of acceptance is made to the offeror or the offeror's agent. In this example the offeree accepted the offer but communication did not make it back to the offeror or the offeror's agent. J's acceptance must be communicated to the seller or the seller's agent.

28. 2 – The Owner cannot access the security deposit until the lease is terminated and possession has been taken. The landlord/owner should charge the tenant for the damage and ensure the repair during the lease term.

29. 3 - In order to test if an item is real or personal property, recall the total circumstance test (IRMA). Personal property becomes a fixture based upon the intention of the party, relationship of the party (owner vs renter), method of attachment and adaptation (customization). Since the hot tub has been wired into the home and attached to the plumbing system it is considered a fixture. When an item is considered a trade fixture it can be removed prior to the expiration of the tenancy. Since the tenant abandoned the property, it becomes a fixture so would no longer be considered a trade fixture when a new tenant moves in.

30. 3 – A borrower can typically avoid private mortgage insurance by making at least a 20% down payment on a conventional loan. VA and FHA loans cannot charge prepayment penalties.

31. 2 – A brokerage is liable for the negligent or willful actions of affiliated brokers. When a broker advertises a property in error, such as wrong square footage, an illegal use based on current zoning or incorrect number of bedrooms, the brokerage cannot disclaim liability.

32. 4 – The determination of negligent or willful actions by a broker can be difficult. In this instance the question does not state that the agent forgot, rather failed to fulfill his or her duties to discover and disclose material facts. The actions by the agent are willful. Since the agent stated something that is not true it is a misrepresentation rather than omission (not saying something). The listing agent has a duty to disclose material facts, regardless of whether the buyer obtains a property inspection. Subrogation is the release of the right to sue in exchange for payment which is obtained when an insurance company pays the loss of an insured party and then will sue the party at fault.

33. 3 – When a broker is granted an exclusive right to represent the buyer they are entitled to compensation regardless of how the buyer was introduced to the property. The broker that writes the offer is typically referred to as the selling broker in an offer to purchase.

34. 4 – A Limited partnership will have at least one general partner and can have multiple limited partners. A limited partner has no direct say in the day to day operations of the entity and liability is limited to the amount invested. S and C Corporations protect investors from personal liability for corporate actions, however a shareholder can vote and have a say in operations.

35. 4 – The landlord receives the fee and therefore has a leased fee interest in the rental property. The tenant has a hold on the premises and therefore the tenant has a leasehold interest in the rental property. When the landlord rents out the

property they have given up the right of possession in return for the rental rate. They do not give up the right of control - they could sell the property to another, subject to the lease agreement.

36. 2 – The calculation is in the name, loan to value, thus loan divided by value. The monthly principal and interest payment is calculated by taking the desired loan and dividing by thousand, then multiplying by the amortization rate. It is important to remember that a bank will loan the lesser of the appraised value or the contract price.

37. 4 – A real estate licensee is not permitted to draft and therefore would not be able to insert multiple unique terms into a contract. The licensee should refer the client to an attorney. The client could elect to write the unique terms into the lease agreements in their own handwriting.

38. 3 – The definition of a condo is the ownership of the airspace of the unit as well as co-ownership of the common areas. When a townhouse is purchased the buyer will own the unit itself as well as the land, with the homeowners association owning the common areas. A co-op means Corporation owned property, where a buyer owns a share of stock and receives a proprietary lease. A planned unit development incorporates multiple types of property - single family, townhouse, condo, as well as commercial activity.

39. 4 – An affiliated broker has the authority to sign listing and buyer agency agreements on behalf of the brokerage, thus forming the agency relationship. The broker in charge is not required to sign to form the agency relationship. Buyers agency agreements may be oral under certain circumstances and therefore would not need to be in writing from inception. An agreement to list property for sale or for rent must be in writing from inception. Representation of a buyer or tenant does not need to be in writing unless the broker/brokerage seeks exclusivity or the buyer tenant desires to make an offer.

40. 3 – A legally binding real estate purchase contract is formed when a written offer has been accepted and notification has been made to the offeror. Since L countered K's offer, L becomes the offeror. When K counters back, he/she becomes the offeror and L is now the offeree. A legally binding contract is formed when L signs the offer and notifies K of acceptance at 10 AM. Earnest money is not required in the contract and unless the contract states that it is time is of the essence, failure to deliver the earnest money would not automatically terminate the purchase contract.

41. 2 – Most loans contain an acceleration clause which allows the lender to call the entire loan balance due, not just the amount of delinquent payments, when a buyer defaults on the mortgage. Due on sale / alienation clause requires the borrower to pay off the entire loan upon sale of the property or separation of ownership (lease option / contract for deed / seller financing). Subordination is trading places, where a lien holder that has a higher lien priority agrees to take a lower priority.

42. 4 – A blanket loan occurs when the lender finances multiple properties / parcels of land into one loan. The loan will require the borrower to pay off a portion of the loan when the borrower sells one of the properties. A "kiddie-condo loan" allows a parent to cosign on a mortgage and most banks allow a parent to cosign a mortgage loan.

43. 4 – When a property value is impacted by outside forces it is known as economic obsolescence. This includes expanding runways at nearby airports, the area becoming more commercial, high voltage power lines or railway service near the property. Function obsolescence relates to issues that are within the property such as poor design, 3 bedrooms and one bath, or outdated style. Highest and best use relates to property valuation and the use that would yield the owner the greatest rate of return. Conformity is a valuation term where an owner will achieve a higher value for the property when it is most similar to surrounding property. A large home will have greater value per square foot when located with other larger homes. A large home surrounded by smaller homes will have a diminished value per square foot.

44. 1 – When a property is financed by a contract for deed or installment land contract the buyer is referred to as the vendee and the seller the vendor. The buyer will have equitable title and the seller legal / actual title in the property until final payment has been made. When a seller provides financing they are not entitled to sue for a deficiency judgement. The seller, under a contract for deed, is permitted to retain all funds paid as well as regaining possession of the property.

45. 1 – A borrower is allowed to lock in an interest rate for a set period of time, this is known as an interest rate lock. The lender will often require the payment of additional funds to extend the rate lock. An extender clause is found in a listing agreement that states that the broker/brokerage is entitled to a commission after the expiration of the listing period when a buyer who was introduced to the property during the listing term decides to purchase the property.

46. 2 – In order to avoid the violation of RESPA (Real Estate Settlement Procedures Act) and the Sherman Anti-Trust Act, a broker / brokerage can provide a buyer with information about service providers, however must disclose that the brokerage has an ownership interest in entities recommended. The buyer is entitled to decide which providers to use.

47. 2 – Real property taxes are charged on real property, not personal property. A manufactured home is considered personal property unless the wheels and hitch are removed, and it is on a permanent foundation on land that is owned. The machinery act allows cities and counties to charge real property taxes based on the assessed value (ad valorem basis).

48. 4 – When a property has been used as a methamphetamine lab it is considered a material fact. It is not a material fact that a seller is behind on the mortgage unless foreclosure notice has been received. It is a violation of fair housing to disclose a handicap such as HIV/AIDS. A property that has been foreclosed on will be advertised as a "foreclosure" property, however the purchaser is not required to disclose to a subsequent buyer how they purchased the home.

49. 3 – A property management agreement will typically authorize the property manager to make repairs below a set dollar amount without having to seek owner approval. In the event that the property is in danger and in need of immediate repair to prevent further damage, the property manager is authorized to make repairs without seeking owner approval. The property manager can bind the principal/owner to lease agreements, however is not able to bind the owner to "ALL" contracts. The property manager can make recommendations to improve the rate of return or value of the property, however cannot make the repairs and then charge the owner. When a property manager is holding the security deposit, it must be held in a trust or escrow account.

50. 4 – An option agreement allows the optionee (buyer) to tie up a property, preventing the optionor (seller) from selling the property to another for a set period of time. The optionee decides whether or not to exercise the option to purchase the property or not exercise the option. An option agreement is deemed to be a unilateral contract until exercised, becoming a bilateral contract. All terms of an option are agreed to up front – purchase price, how the option is to be exercised, whether the option fee is credited at closing, and how the long the optionee has to exercise the option.

51. 3 – The law of conformity states that homes retain a higher value when they are most similar to other neighboring properties. A large home surrounded by smaller homes will have a diminished value per square foot. A small home surrounded by larger homes will typically have a higher value per square foot.

52. 3 – The Federal Fair Housing Act allows a tenant to modify the rental premises at the tenant's expense to make a property handicap accessible. There are limited exceptions to the law for a seller so long as they do not use discriminatory advertising or tell the individual why they are refusing to rent. An owner is exempt when leasing a multifamily property with four or fewer units, where one of the units is owner occupied, senior housing, owner of 3 or fewer homes – selling no more

than one home every two years, private clubs and religious organizations. It is important to note that a realtor can never discriminate and an owner that hires a realtor loses the above exemptions.

53. 4 – The Federal Fair Housing Act permits the owner of an owner occupied rental property up to four units to discriminate against the protected classes so long as a real estate agent is not hired, the owner does not discriminate in advertising, and the owner does not state why they are refusing to rent.

54. 4 – Earnest money is not required in a contract. Consideration is required, and is met by the mutual promises between the buyer and seller, where the buyer agrees to buy and the seller agrees to sell at the agreed upon purchase price. Acknowledgement occurs when a notary notarizes a signature on an official document like a deed or power of attorney. It is not required for a purchase transaction.

55. 1 – The Sherman Antitrust Act does not allow price fixing or boycotting. A buyer is permitted to select service providers in the transaction and a real estate broker cannot refuse to work with that individual/entity. Since total compensation is disclosed to the prospective buyer, there is no requirement to disclose the amount paid for a referral fee. In addition, a real estate broker would not be permitted to state that the commission charged to a buyer or seller is "usual", "customary" or "what everyone charges".

56. 3 – While a salesperson/broker can call a client with a previous business relationship within the past 18-months, the salesperson did not have a prior business relationship with the seller. Other exceptions include invitation or personal relationship.

57. 1 – When new business relocates in a city it will increase demand for available housing, thus increasing property values. When inventory levels increase, without a corresponding increase in demand, prices will fall. Interest rate increases will cause the cost of home ownership to rise and reduce demand. When an area becomes more commercial around a particular property, which can case pollution, it is common for residential property values to fall.

58. 1 – The Can-Spam act restricts the ability to send unsolicited emails and require a prominent opt-out to be displayed. There are very few limitations for sending unsolicited mail through the US Postal Service.

59. 3 – When a property is auctioned it is common for the lender to bid the amount that the buyer currently owes. The lender does not have to keep auctioning the property until the bid is higher than the amount currently owed. Many foreclosure properties are "under water", meaning that the borrower owes more than the property is worth.

60. 2 - The premium for a title insurance policy is paid once at the time of closing. There are no annual premiums that are required to be paid subsequent to closing. There are standard and extended policies available, with extended being the preferred policy as it covers the buyer against more potential losses. The borrower will typically pay for both the lender/mortgagee policy and borrower/mortgagor policy.

61. 4 – The exclusive right to sell listing agreement is binding between the firm and the client. The firm can appoint another broker to fulfill the terms of the agreement in the unfortunate circumstance of death, insanity or the broker that signed the agreement resigns.

62. 3 – When a tenant signed a net lease, they pay monthly rent plus property tax, insurance and/or common area maintenance. A gross lease requires the tenant to pay monthly rent and the owner to pay property tax, insurance and/or common area maintenance fees. A percentage lease is often used in retail rental agreements where the tenant pays a low flat rental plus a percentage of sales to the landlord. A ground lease requires the tenant to pay rent for the land as well as pay for the construction cost of the building, which is often an extended lease (ex: 99 year lease with a 99 year renewal).

63. 3 – A property manager or owner would not be permitted to discriminate against families with small children under the federal fair housing act. A property manager or owner can refuse to rent when a family is too large for the apartment, the tenant has had past rental difficulty (evicted for nonpayment or damages), or the tenant does not have sufficient income to meet the credit guidelines apply to all prospective tenants.

64. 4 – A property manager is typically not authorized to make changes to the property, even when the changes may result in increased rent. The owner of the property would have to authorize those changes. A property manager is often entrusted to hold repair funds on behalf of the owner. They would not be permitted to deficit spend, spending more than the amount paid by the property owner, even if they have additional funds in the account. Trust account money is other people's money. The property manager can expend his or her own funds and invoice the owner for the HVAC repair.

65. 2 – Regulation Z governs financial disclosures when an individual/entity runs an ad regarding consumer finance. Trigger terms include the amount of down payment expressed as a percentage or dollar amount, the amount of any payment, the number of payments, the period of repayment or the amount of finance charges. Use of one of the trigger terms requires disclosure of all of the terms plus the annual percentage rate. It is important to remember that APR alone does not trigger full disclosure. A broker can use general terms such as easy monthly

payments, low down payment or great financing available without triggering the disclosure requirement.

66. 1 – When a seller refuses to authorize dual agency, the listing agent and/or the listing agent's company would not be permitted to represent the buyer. The buyer would be considered a 3rd party, which the listing agent owes honesty, fairness and disclosure of material facts. The listing agent has no duty to determine if the property will meet the buyer's needs. When a buyer discloses his/her intended use of the property, the listing agent should recommend the buyer to investigate the use or refer the buyer to an attorney. The listing agent can provide unadjusted sales data to the buyer, however cannot prepare a comparative market analysis as this could weaken the sellers bargaining position. The listing agent owes the seller the duty of confidentiality and therefore should not disclose that the seller will accept less than the list price.

67. 3 – Directing or channeling a buyer to particular neighborhoods based on one or more of the protected classes under the federal fair housing act is known as steering. Redlining was a common practice of refusing to lend or insure loans in racially mixed areas. Blockbusting is defined as inducing the sale of property because one of the protected classes are moving into the neighborhood.

68. 4 – The Lead Based Paint Addendum is used in most homes built prior to 1978. Disclosure is required in residential sales, so if the property has been converted to commercial there is no disclosure requirement.

69. 3 – A property that is under contract however has not closed is considered executory. It is common to test on other "e" words, such as execute (which means to sign) and executed (which means completed or closed). A buyer holds equitable title until a property has been purchased. The question does not state if the property is located in a title theory or lien theory state, and it is important not to read into the question. In a title theory state the borrower would retain equitable title in the lender would hold legal title after closing. In a lien theory state the borrower would gain legal title after closing and the lender would hold equitable title.

70. 2 – A suit to quiet title or action to quiet title is used when there is a dispute about who holds legal title to the property or has the greatest claim. Adverse possession occurs when a party hostilely and intentionally takes the property of another and the taking is open, continuous, exclusive, adverse and notorious. The right of redemption is available when a property is being foreclosed on. The equitable right of redemption is the right of the owner to pay off the liens prior to the foreclosure sale. The statutory right of redemption is the right of the owner to pay off the liens prior to the finalizing of the foreclosure sale (10-day period in North Carolina). Eminent domain is the government's right to take private property for the public good. The owner must be compensated fair market value.

71. 4 – When an individual is acting under a power of attorney or as an attorney in fact, they are acting as a universal agent. A universal agent has all-encompassing powers to legally bind an individual to a contract. When a broker represents a buyer, seller or tenant they act as special agents. A special agent has no signing authority and is limited to gathering and presenting information. When a broker affiliates with a brokerage under an independent contractor agreement or enters into a property management agreement they will act as general agents. A general agent is limited to certain defined tasks such as finding tenants and signing lease agreements on behalf of an owner, however is not authorized to sell the property or make changes.

72. 4 – The best course of action when a homeowner is violating restrictive/protective covenants is to file a complaint with the homeowner's association. Since this is not an option in the question, the second-best answer is seeking an injunction through the courts. The local housing department and police department will not hear a complaint unless it is a violation of law. It is not advisable to encourage neighbors to send letters demanding a neighbor to stop a certain action.

73. 1 – When a lender agrees to take a lower priority it is known as subordination. Disintermediation is direct investing rather than passing through a middle man such as a real estate investment trust. Affirmation is the continuation of a void or voidable contract through closing, thus affirming it is legally binding.

74. 2 – The metes and bounds system is used in the 13 original colonies. The rest of the country uses the government rectangular survey system. It is important to remember that a township has 36 sections, there are 640 acres in a section and that section 16 is where the school is typically located. The principal meridian runs north to south and the base line runs east to west. It is common practice for real estate brokers to reference recorded legal documents such as deed book and page / plat book and page, property tax ID and other legal description. The deed will contain all of these items as well as the metes and bounds or government rectangular survey system description.

75. 2 – Current market conditions will always have the greatest impact when establishing a list price. A broker will typically look at past sales to establish a recommended price range, however if market conditions sharply improve or worsen it can have a dramatic impact on the probable sales price. A property sold for sale by owner is typically not a good comp as the property wasn't made for sale on the open market. A seller may have unreasonable expectations regarding how much they will net from the sale of a property.

76. 2 – A licensee owes a customer honesty, fairness and disclosure of material facts. A licensee owes a client obedience, loyalty, disclosure, confidentiality, accounting and reasonable skill, care and diligence.

77. 4 – Property taxes and local public assessments have the highest priority in a foreclosure sale over other recorded liens. A mechanics lien can jump in priority to the first day labor or materials were provided assuming it has met the statutory requirements. The first mortgage is often the first recorded lien against a property. A federal income tax lien is a general lien against all property and does not take priority over other recorded liens.

78. 4 – A percentage lease is often used in retail where the tenant pays a low base rent and a percentage of sales to the owner. A full service lease will typically include other services, such as cleaning or security, which the landlord agrees to provide. A gross lease, is a flat or level lease where the tenant pays the landlord and the landlord remains responsible for the costs of ownership (taxes, insurance, common area maintenance).

79. 4 – Net operating income is calculated by taking effective gross income and subtracting operating expenses (no depreciation, debt service or capital improvements). Effective gross income, also known as total anticipated revenue, is calculated by taking gross income and subtracting vacancy and collection losses. The capitalization rate is calculated when you divide net operating income by the value of a property.

80. 2 – A lease agreement that automatically renews for successive periods unless a party gives notice is known as a periodic estate or estate from year to year. An estate for years has a definite end date and will terminate without notice.

81. 4 – A special use permit allows a property owner to use a property for a specific use that does not follow the current zoning in that area. It is provided for in long-term planning and is in the public's interest (such as low income housing, hospitals, museums, etc.). A variance is a minor change to the property. Spot zoning is changing the rules for one property rather than the surrounding area typically for the financial benefit of the owner. There is no such thing as a subsequent exception permit.

82. 2 – A licensee/broker should verify the owner of record by checking with the register of deeds office. While the licensee may talk to the attorney handling the estate, they still need to check the public record. A release of title is the release of a lien once final payment has been made.

83. 3 – A seller cannot modify the amount of compensation outlined in the listing agreement without firm approval. The seller could use a net listing to help the seller achieve his or her goal for net proceeds. Net listings are not common in general practice.

84. 2 – The Sheriff's Department does not handle complaints regarding deed restrictions as this is a matter for the courts. Deed restrictions run with the land and are therefore binding upon future owners. They are typically more restrictive then

current zoning regulations and "may" or "may not" result of the automatic loss of the property.

85. 2 – Since we are calculating the required sales price to net the seller $30,000 we are only concerned about seller debits and credits. Since property taxes have been paid for the year by the seller, the buyer will need to reimburse the seller for the period of time the buyer will own the property.

The first step is to calculate the seller known debits and credits. We now know all expenses the seller will pay EXCEPT for commission and the commission paid is based on the sales price (which we are solving for. We know that the seller must pay 6%, so if the sales price is 100% and commission is 6%, all other known expenses is 94%. When you divide the known expenses by 94%, you will calculate the sale price.

Seller knowns: $125,000 loan + $1,400 seller closing costs - $276.20 tax proration credit to seller + $125 deed prep + $30,000 seller required net = $156,248.80
Knowns as % of sales price: 100% - 6% commission = 94%
Sales Price: $156,248.80 ÷ 94% = $166,222.22, rounded to $166,200

Tax Proration – buyer days: (O) 12 + (ND) 60 = 72 Days
Tax Proration – daily rate: $1,381 ÷ 360 = $3.8361
Tax Proration - $3.8361 X 72 days = $276.20 (debit buyer / credit seller)

86. 1 – When you calculate the square footage of a lot, you multiply the length X the width. The problem gives the square footage and the depth of the lot. This is calculated by taking the square footage and dividing it by the depth.

Lot 1 Front Feet: 187,500 ÷ 250 = 750
Lot 2 Front Feet: 112,500 ÷ 250 = 450
Total front footage: 750 + 250 = 1,200

87. 3 – It is important to remember how many square feet are in an acres: 4 blue haired ladies going 35 in a 60, or 43,560 square feet in an acre.

Lot Square Footage: 4,500 X 1,800 = 8,100,000
Acres: 8,100,000 ÷ 43,560 = 185.95041 acres
Probable Sales Price: 185.95041 X $45,000 = $8,367,768

88. 2 – The first step is calculating the amount of the loan, then dividing the loan amount by 3.

Bank Loan: $315,000 - $45,000 = $270,000
Gross Income: $270,000 ÷ 3 = $90,000

89. 1 – Property taxes are charged per $1,000 of the assessed value when using the mills rate method. Property taxes for the year are calculated by taking the assessed value, dividing by 1,000, then multiplying by the mills rate. This question has the added trick of asking for "monthly" tax liability. To calculate the monthly amount, divide the annual tax by 12.

Assessed Value: $280,000 X 70% = $196,000
Tax for Year: $196,000 ÷ 1,000 X 18 mills = $3,528
Monthly Tax: $3,528 ÷ 12 = $294

90. 2 – The "selling agent" represents the buyer (or writes up the offer as the seller subagent). In this problem, the selling agent is the buyer's agent. Compensation between the listing and selling agent is split, with each receiving 4%. Commission splits are typically quoted as the amount paid to the agent, followed by the amount paid to the firm. Commission is based on the sales price of the property.

Total Commission Selling Side: $245,000 X 4% = $9,800
Selling Agent Commission: $9,800 X 70 % = $6,860

91. 3 – To calculate the percentage gain or loss you must first determine the amount of gain or loss (new – old). To calculate the percentage, divide the gain or loss by the old amount. New means the current value and old means the original purchase price.

Total Lot Sales: $35,000 X 8 = $280,000
Gain: $280,000 new - $75,000 old = $205,000
Percentage Gain: $205,000 ÷ $75,000 = 2.7333 or 273%

92. 3 – The value of a property using the direct capitalization method is calculated by taking the NOI and dividing by the capitalization rate. When calculating net operating income it is important to remember the following:

Gross Income – Vacancy & Collection = Effective Gross Income
Effective Gross Income – Operating Expenses = Net Operating Income

Effective gross income (also called Total Anticipated Revenue) is often used as a distractor in a problem that provides it and states the vacancy & collection loss. Most students will subtract vacancy & collection losses a second time, resulting in an incorrect answer. Do not included depreciation, debt service nor capital improvements in operating expenses.

Net Operating Income: $120,000 EGI - $10,000 mgt fee - $8,000 other operating = $102,000
Value: $102,000 NOI ÷ 15% = $680,000

93. 4 – To calculate annual taxes using the mills rate, recall the following formula:

Annual Taxes: Assessed Value ÷ 1,000 X Mills Rate

In this problem, we are solving for the mills rate. You can use the T-bar to calculate the answer or memorize the following formula:

Mills Rate: Annual Property Tax ÷ (Assessed Value ÷ 1,000)

Annual taxes: $217.30 X 12 = $2,607.60
Mills Rate: $2,607.60 ÷ (175,000 ÷ 1,000) = 14.9

94. 2 – The area of a triangle is calculated by taking 1/2 (Base X Height). While this problem does not contain unheated square footage (stoop, garage, porch, etc.), it is important to recall that they would not be considered living area. Living area must be heated, finished and directly accessible.

Area of Rectangle: 65' X 30' = 1,950 sqft
Area of Triangle: 1/2 (30' X 30') = 450
Total Living Area Square Footage: 1,950 + 450 = 2,400

95. 4 – To calculate the remaining value of a building using the cost approach, first calculate the cost of the building new, then back out depreciation (often using the straight-line method, and then add in the cost of land/improvements. Note that economic life is another term for useful life. The actual age is a distractor (not needed to solve the problem); recall that it is not your actual age, it is how you act (effective age) that matters.

Cost New: 4,500 sqft X $110 = $495,000   Cost ÷ Econ life x eff. Li G
Depreciation: $495,000 ÷ 75 yrs X 5 = $33,000
Value: $495,000 new - $33,000 depreciation + $55,000 = $517,000

N – O ÷ O (comp)

96. 3 – The gross rent multiplier is calculated by taking the sales price and dividing by the monthly gross rent. It is important to read the question for the number of units, as rent is often quoted as an amount per unit (duplex = 2 units, triplex = 3 units, etc.).

Gross Month Rent: $750 X 3 = $2,250
Gross Rent Multiplier: $180,000 ÷ $2,250 = 80

97. 2 – When working qualifying loan problems, first break monthly debt obligations into housing expenses (principal, interest, taxes, insurance, HOA dues) and total debt (housing expense + recurring debt obligations). For this problem, it is only necessary to calculate the total debt ratio, as we are calculating the amount of addition debt a borrower can have and still qualify for the loan.

Recurring debt obligations with 5 or fewer monthly payments remaining are considered short-term and therefore not included as recurring obligations. Recurring debt obligations with 6 or more monthly payments are considered long-term and therefore included as recurring obligations. Conventional loan limits for testing purposes are 28% housing expense and 36% total debt (housing expense and recurring obligations).

Monthly Income: $150,000 ÷ 12 = $12,500
Maximum Total Debt: $12,500 X 36% = $4,500

PITI Payment: $2,150 PI + $600 T + $50 I = $2,800
Additional Debt: $4,500 Max - $2,800 PITI - $650 Car = $1,050

Note: The student loan matures in 5 months, so it is considered short-term.

98. 3 – For this problem, you must work backwards from before tax cash flow and calculate the property's effective gross income. Since vacancy & collection are 5%, this means that EGI is 95% of Gross Income. To calculate the annual gross income, divide effective gross income by 95%. The problem can state annual or monthly rent per unit. For this problem, you only need to calculate gross annual rent per unit.

Before Tax Cash Flow (BTCF) is calculated as follows:

Gross Income – Vacancy & Collection = Effective Gross Income
Effective Gross Income – Operating Expenses – Debt Service = BTCF

Effective Gross Income: $750,000 BTCF + $75,000 Debt Service + $50,000 Property Tax + $100,000 Management Fees = $975,000 *EGI*
Effective Gross Income Percentage: GI 100% - V&C 5% = 95%

EGI   5% &100%

Gross Income: $975,000 ÷ 95% = $1,026,315.70
Gross Income per Unit: $1,026,315.70 ÷ 100 = $10,263.15 or rounded $10,260

\ unit

99. 2 – When calculating the seller's net, it is important to recall the expenses that the seller is typically pays C, D and E – commission, deed prep and excise tax, with the buyer paying most other expenses unless otherwise stated. The seller is typically responsible for paying the mortgage cancellation / mortgage satisfaction / satisfaction of mortgage recording fee. Since the seller paid the entire year of property taxes, they buyer needs to reimburse the seller for the number of days they are responsible. Note that the problem states that the buyer is responsible for the day of closing for taxes.

Sellers Net: $300,000 SP - $199,800 Loan Payoff - $45 Mtg Cancellation -

$21,000 Commission - $125 Deed Prep - $4,000 Closing Costs + $902.89 Tax Proration = $75,932.89, rounded $75,933

Commission: $300,000 X 7% = $21,000

Tax Proration – Buyer Days: (O) 8 + (ND) 60 = 68 days
Tax Proration - Daily Rate: $4,780 ÷ 360 = $13.2777
Tax Proration – Entry: $13.2777 X 68 = $902.89 Debit Buyer / Credit Seller

100. 2 – When calculating the amount the buyer will need to bring to closing, it helps to remember what the seller typically pays and that the buyer will pay the remainder. Seller typically pays commission, deed prep, excise tax and mortgage cancellation fees. It is important to remember that items that are paid outside closing have already been paid for and therefore do not impact the amount of funds needed to close. When calculating the number of days to charge interim interest, subtract the day of closing from 30, then add 1 day because the bank is greedy.

Since the closing is before September 1 and taxes are unpaid, the entry on the settlement statement would be debit the seller / credit the buyer. Since the buyer will pay the day of closing, subtract a day from the total seller days.

Discount points and origination fees are charged as a percentage of the loan amount, not the purchase price.

Buyer Due at Closing: $180,000 SP - $162,000 Loan - $3,000 EMD + $1,620 Orig Fee + $3,240 Disc Pnt + $455.63 Interim/Prepaid Interest + $800 Attorney Fee - $315 Tax Proration = $20,800.63, rounded $20,801

Interim Interest – Days: 30 - 4 + 1 = 27 days
Interim Interest – Loan Amount: $180,000 x 90% = $162,000
Interim Interest – Daily Rate: $162,000 X 3.75% ÷ 360 = $16.875
Interim Interest Charge: $16.875 X 27 days = $455.63

Origination Fee: $162,000 X 1% = $1,620
Discount Points: $162,000 X 2% = $3,240

Tax Proration – Buyer Days: (JF) 60 + (M) 3 = 63 days
Tax Proration - Daily Rate: $1,800 ÷ 360 = $15
Tax Proration – Entry: $5 X 63 = $315 Debit Seller / Credit Buyer

Check out our other products at:

www.3WiseTeachers.com

Available Now

Real Estate Prelicense
Math Workbook

2017 - 2018

Matt Davies

Doug Sinclair

Tiffany Stiles

First Edition

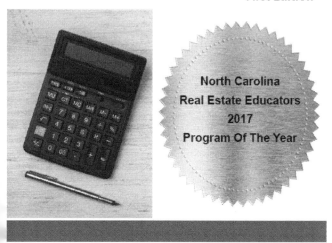

North Carolina
Real Estate Educators
2017
Program Of The Year

Available Now

North Carolina Real Estate
State Only Exam Review

2017 - 2018

Matt Davies

Tiffany Stiles

First Edition

3 Wise Teachers

Made in the USA
San Bernardino, CA
04 September 2017